Planning to teach Science in the Primary Classroom

KS1 & KS2

Rachel Sparks Linfield

HOPSCOTCH
A division of MA Education Ltd

Published by
Hopscotch, a division of MA Education,
St Jude's Church, Dulwich Road,
London, SE24 0PB
www.hopscotchbooks.com
020 7738 5454

© 2009 MA Education Ltd.

Written by Rachel Sparks Linfield

Illustrated by Emma Squire,
Fonthill Creative, 01722 717057

ISBN 978 1 90539 073 1

All rights reserved. This resource is sold subject to the condition that it shall not, by way of trade or otherwise, be lent, hired out or otherwise circulated without the publisher's prior consent in any form of binding or cover other than that in which it is published and without a similar condition, including this condition, being imposed upon the subsequent purchaser.

No part of this publication may be reproduced, stored in a retrieval system, or transmitted, in any form or by any means, electronic, mechanical, photocopying, recording or otherwise, without the prior permission of the publisher, except where photocopying for educational purposes within the school or other educational establishment that has purchased this book is expressly permitted in the text.

Every effort has been made to trace the owners of copyright of material in this book and the publisher apologises for any inadvertent omissions. Any persons claiming copyright for any material should contact the publisher who will be happy to pay the permission fees agreed between them and who will amend the information in this book on any subsequent reprint.

Contents

Introduction 6

Section 1 7
What is science?
What are concepts?
What is scientific investigation?
Fair testing and controlling variables
Planning for science
When should technical vocabulary be introduced?
Recording in science
Creative records
Assessing science
Using ICT
Using cross-curricular links
Displays
Catering for individual needs

Section 2 14
Science Activities for Key Stages 1 and 2
Developing skills
Activity levels
Safety
- Safety when working with plants
- Safety when pond dipping

Activities to teach Life and Living Things 15
- Life processes
- Humans and other animals
- Senses
- Teeth
- Exercise and healthy diets
- Hearts
- Skeletons
- Life cycles
- Drugs
- Green plants
- Variation and classification
- Living things in their environment
- Feeding relationships
- Micro-organisms

Activities to teach Materials 20
- Grouping and classifying materials
- Keeping warm
- Rocks and soils
- Solids, liquids and gases
- Changing materials
- Temperature
- Non-reversible changes
- Separating mixtures of materials

Activities to teach Energy, Movement and Forces 23
- Electricity
- Forces and motion
- Magnets
- Friction
- Forces in action and measuring forces
- Light and dark
- Shadows
- Reflecting light and seeing
- Making and detecting sounds
- Changing sounds and hearing
- The Sun, Earth and Moon
- Periodic changes

Section 3 28
Background knowledge for teachers:
- Life processes and cells
- Plants
- Atoms
- Solids, liquids and gases
- Forces
- Magnets
- Energy
- Electricity
- Light
- Sound

Glossary for Life and Living Things
Glossary for Materials
Glossary for Energy, Movement and Forces

Section 4 32
Copy Masters
CM1 Planning an investigation
CM2 Plant parts
CM3 Human digestive system
CM4 Human body skeleton
CM5 Inside the human eye and ear
CM6 Human teeth
CM7 Living or never been alive?
CM8 Where do minibeasts live?
CM9 Balanced eating
CM10 Identifying leaves
CM11 Identifying plants
CM12 Identifying minibeasts
CM13 Identifying pond creatures
CM14 Making paper 'seeds'
CM15 Germinating seed flick book
CM16 Gas, liquid or solid
CM17 Make a circuit
CM18 Ideas for making musical instruments
CM19 Making a glossary
CM20 Did you know?

Table with links to the QCA Units of Work for Science 52

Index 53

Introduction

As a child I first became interested in science when, aged nine, my teacher showed me that if I stood one metre away from a mirror my mirror image was one metre behind. This fascinated me and so began many hours of investigating. When shopping with my mother I loved to try and trick the department store mirrors. I would stand in front of mirrors and see whether I could 'catch out' my reflection. I would ask lots of questions such as 'Is the reflection in the mirror or behind it?' 'Does the metre 'rule' work with all mirrors?' 'Does the thickness of the mirror matter?' 'What happens if the mirror is made from plastic?'

For me science was, and still is today, about finding out why things happen and how things work. It is about developing understanding of our world and realising how different factors affect what happens. It is about asking questions, researching ideas, carrying out practical investigations and interpreting results. Most importantly science gives us the opportunity to develop a wide range of skills and to use our imaginations as we try to make sense of what we observe, read and are told.

The majority of children have an instinctive desire to investigate and to explore. Babies will shake, feel, lick and look at rattles. Over time they begin to form preferences for a particular toy perhaps based on its feel, sound or smell. Other toys will be rejected. In making these choices, babies and toddlers begin to develop the ability to make observations. Young children frequently ask 'Why?'. When they wonder why a battery toy stops working, how to make a loud noise with a drum or try to build a tall tower of toy bricks, they are developing the ability to enquire, to ask questions and to explore. These key, early skills are excellent preparation for taught science in school. Teachers thus must appreciate that children have already had many relevant, prior experiences, before they are ever taught science in school.

Planning to Teach Science in the Primary Classroom has been written for trainees, supply teachers and non-specialist science teachers to help with the planning, teaching and assessing of science. It provides information about the key characteristics of science that should be developed within teaching and learning, and explains how to plan for, teach and assess science. It gives ideas for activities for the concept areas given within the National Curriculum for Science at Key Stages 1 and 2 and, also, gives children the opportunity to plan and carry out their own investigations. Where appropriate, teacher subject knowledge is supplied. Copy Masters provide diagrams for topics such as the human body and parts of a plant; sheets to plan investigations and a balanced meal; sheets to identify plants, leaves, minibeasts and pond creatures and a 'Did you know?' fact sheet to promote discussion and stimulate interest in science. A tracking sheet shows how the given activities in Section 2 relate to the 'QCA Scheme of Work for Science'.

Planning to Teach Science in the Primary Classroom does not set out to be a scheme of work. Instead the intention is to have a flexible resource to 'dip into' at the planning stage. It can be used as the initial place for ideas when planning a scheme of work or to support existing school schemes of work or ones such as the QCA Scheme of Work for Science. Quality planning, teaching and learning in science must reflect the interests and abilities of the children.

Section 1

What is Science?
Science may be thought of as comprising of two elements: concepts/ideas and processes/skills. Consideration for both elements must be given when planning for teaching and learning in science.

What are concepts?
Concepts are the 'big ideas'. For example, to understand the concept of floating and sinking a number of smaller ideas need to be developed and understood. We need to know that things float if they are light for their size and have an awareness of the properties of materials.

To have a concept of magnetism we need to be aware of key ideas such as all magnets have two magnetic poles, that like poles repel and unlike poles attract and that iron, steel, nickel and cobalt are attracted by magnets.

A key way to develop ideas in science is to carry out experiments and investigations. Sometimes these will simply be to illustrate a point. At other times they will be to research ideas and gather data. It must be stressed that although some science inevitably is learnt through secondary sources such as the internet, books and CD ROMs it is vital that, wherever possible, practical experiments and investigations take place.

What is scientific investigation?

Scientific investigation involves using a variety of processes to answer questions and gather data. Processes include aspects such as predicting, observing and recording. Within each process there are a number of related skills whose level of difficulty and sophistication will vary according to the age and ability of the scientist. For example, the process of measuring includes using non-standard and standard measures. It involves using a range of instruments to measure length, mass, weight, capacity, temperature and so on.

The process begins to develop when children make simple comparisons such as 'Edmund's parachute fell quicker than Leanne's.' The process is refined when standard measurements are introduced. Later on measurements will be taken a number of times and averaged to determine experimental errors. Not only do children need to be given the opportunity to practise and develop the various skills, they also need to understand when to choose to use a particular skill.

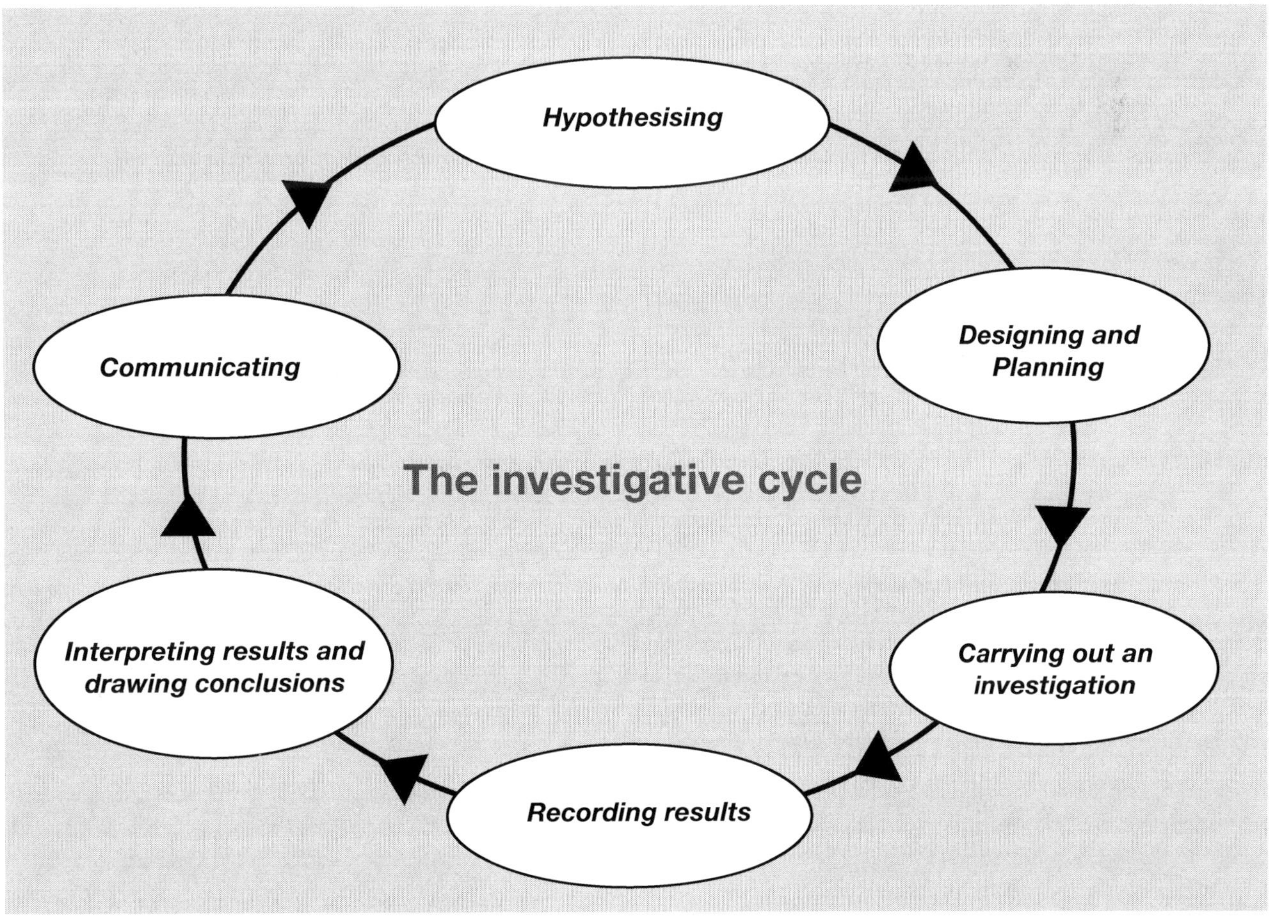

The investigative cycle

- Hypothesising
- Designing and Planning
- Carrying out an investigation
- Recording results
- Interpreting results and drawing conclusions
- Communicating

Planning to teach Science in the Primary Classroom

Section One 7

Regardless of the age of the scientist, the scientific investigative cycle is the same. It involves identifying an area to study; having an idea; finding a question to investigate; researching the idea through practical experience and/or secondary sources; recording and communicating findings; comparing the findings with the original idea and predictions and, if necessary, refining ideas. The cycle is shown in the diagram on the previous page.

It will not always be appropriate for the children to undertake the whole cycle. Sometimes a teacher might wish the class to focus on an aspect such as selecting equipment; finding the question; planning a fair test or making observations. Also, it must be remembered that carrying out the whole cycle requires quality time both for thinking and doing. Several lessons may be needed for a full investigation. During a year, however, teachers should plan for children to experience all parts of the investigative cycle.

Fair tests and controlling variables

Fair testing is one of science's distinctive processes. It involves controlling variables, the 'things' that might make a difference to how something behaves, reacts or grows. In a scientific investigation to discover how seeds germinate best we might want to consider the effects of the variables light and water. To make the investigation fair we would need to keep other variables constant. We would have to use the same number and type of seeds (e.g. cress); the same size and type of pots and the same growing medium (e.g. cotton wool). We could then place a pot with water and one without in a dark cupboard and two similar pots on a windowsill. If children looked at the pots each day and ensured the ones with water were always wet it would be possible to carry out a fair test and to discover the best conditions for germinating seeds.

> *When planning fair tests children should be encouraged to be critical*

In the early days of planning fair tests children will need support. Some children will have an everyday concept of 'fair' such as, 'It was fair, I had one go then Lucy had the other'. These children need to be helped to go beyond the idea of fair as 'taking turns' to controlling variables. Starting at an early age, however, listing the factors that could be changed to make a difference will help children to be able to plan fair tests. It is also important that they are aware that tests may not always be entirely fair. For instance, in the seeds germinating example, the temperature in the cupboard and on the windowsill may not have been the same. When dropping paper parachutes of various sizes, despite controlling variables such as the way they are dropped, the material for the parachutes and the shape, changing the size of the parachute also effects the mass of the parachutes. Thus, when planning fair tests, children should be encouraged to be critical and to appreciate that it may be very difficult to control all the variables.

A good way to help children to plan fair tests is to use Copy Master 1. It could be printed on to A3 sized paper or reproduced for an interactive whiteboard. The sheet asks the children to consider all the things that could be changed to make a difference. For example for a plant investigation the children could change the amount of light, the growing medium, the amount of water, the temperature and the types of seed. Each factor could be written on a sticky note and placed in one of the boxes. The children then have to decide which of the factors they would like to investigate and, as a result, which they will keep the same. From this stage it is then a simple matter to form a precise question to investigate such as 'Will the amount of water given to the plant affect the height?' The sheet helps children to be precise in their use of language and helps them to avoid saying 'best' without clarification.

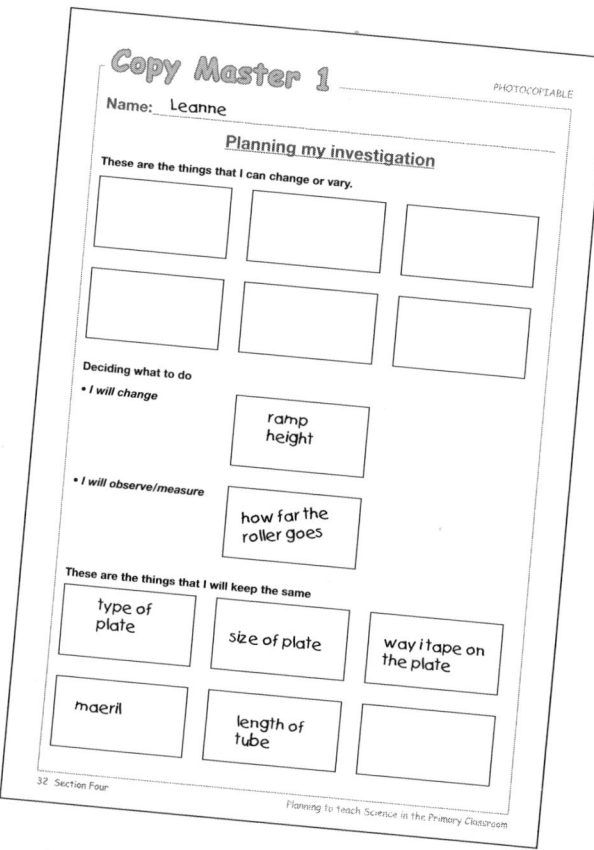

The illustration above shows a completed sheet for a class asked to consider a roller made from two paper plates attached to a cardboard tube that would be released down a ramp. The Year 2 class was asked what they could change to make a difference to how far the roller went.

In some schools children are encouraged to use the terms 'dependent' and 'independent' variable. In this case, an 'independent variable' is what will be changed in an investigation. The 'dependent variable' is what is observed or measured.

Planning for science

Documents such as National Curricula and the 'QCA Science Scheme of Work' provide general headings and 'Learning Intentions' on which to base school, Key Stage and class schemes of work. It is important that schemes for a given class take into account the interests of the children, their prior learning, their abilities and the age appropriate conceptual and investigational skill content. Schemes should consider extension and support, allowing each child to consolidate knowledge and to develop ideas and understanding. Thought should also be given to links to other curriculum areas, resources, safety and key vocabulary.

Session plans that involve practical activities must outline safety concerns. It is often stressed that much of primary science can be taught with everyday resources. It is important though to realise that some everyday materials found commonly around the home may not be appropriate for use in school. For example, some parts of common garden plants may be poisonous or cause allergic reactions. When planning any practical science activity, school and area safety guidelines should be followed. Teachers must ensure that appropriate risk assessments are in place. 'Be Safe' published by the Association for Science Education provides invaluable support on matters of safety (see *http://www.ase.org.uk*).

Session plans should outline the learning intentions in 'child-speak'. Children need to know what the purpose of the lesson is and what they might hope to learn. The introduction to a lesson must set out these goals and also the context for the lesson. For example, if the concept is 'to know which materials can be attracted by a magnet', the children need to have a reason for finding this out such as choosing a material to make a magnetic game. Discovering which papers are absorbent is irrelevant if the facts are not related to real life, such as finding something to mop up spills. Learning about healthy diets is far more interesting when it involves making healthy sandwiches for a person, function or fictional character as opposed to simply sorting foods within a table. Carefully chosen contexts can not only motivate children but also lead them to want to experiment, to investigate and to research ideas independently at home.

The central part of the lesson will often involve practical work. During a year there should be a balance of adult-led and child-initiated activity. Sometimes practical activity is to illustrate a skill or idea and might be a teacher demonstration or involve the children following a set procedure. At other times the children should have the opportunity to plan what to do and to record, and to select their own equipment. The choice of whether to work alone, in pairs small groups, or as a class will depend on the available equipment, time constraints and the topic area. Ideally, over the course of a year, arrangements for practical work should allow each child to develop their scientific skills and conceptual understanding using the full range of teaching and learning contexts. The children should also be encouraged to consider why they are doing the science in a particular way; they should understand when independent, paired, group or class work is appropriate or why a teacher has chosen to demonstrate an experiment rather than allow the children, themselves, to investigate.

Plenaries, where a class comes together to share their findings, are a common feature of the majority of lessons carried out in primary classrooms. Sometimes, however, plenaries can either degenerate into 'clearing up times' or de-motivating 'show and tell' times where once a child or group has shown their findings they lose interest. It is important that session plans should consider ways to vary the organisation and content of plenaries to keep all the children interested and make them a valuable part of the scientific learning process.

When should technical language be introduced?

Within science there are a vast number of key words which have both common sense and scientific meanings. For example, in science a 'force' is a 'push or a pull'. Yet in everyday life the word is used in phrases such as 'my mum forces me to do this' and 'Air Force'. Non-fiction science books for Key Stage 2 children often have glossaries containing vocabulary such as 'anther', carpel' and 'nucleus'. This can create the impression that such words are vital for science and many children throughout England, in recent years, have had to learn huge amounts of vocabulary for end of Key Stage tests. As teachers, though, we must ask two key questions before introducing a technical word:
- Have the children had experience of the word?

- Will using the scientific vocabulary help the children to clarify their ideas and increase their understanding?

Appropriate scientific vocabulary should allow children to communicate and to explain. When the children are introduced to technical, scientific vocabulary ample opportunity should be given to use the words. The use of games can help children to build their scientific vocabularies. For example, 'lotto boards' could be made with words associated with properties of materials and definitions can be read out. Alternatively, children can be given words and then go on treasure hunts to find their definitions. Class science dictionaries can be made where the children suggest the words to include and, also, help to supply the definitions. Copy Master 18 provides a grid for children to make their own glossaries of scientific words. Glossaries for teachers are provided in Section 3. Teachers may wish to use some of the given definitions with the children.

It is vital that teachers listen closely to how the children and, also, adults in the classroom, including themselves, use everyday words, scientific words and phrases. For example, a common phrase heard when classes are using magnets is 'The paperclip is sticking to the magnet.' This is a time when the word 'attracted' would be far more beneficial. The word 'stick' creates a misconception of a 'glue-like' effect. When teaching about day and night, care should be taken when describing the movement of the Earth. The Earth spins around its axis and orbits around the Sun. Teachers with younger children such as in the five to seven age range, will often hear children using words in incorrect contexts. Magnets, for example, are said to 'magnify paperclips'. Listening to what children say and being aware of the example we set as teachers is of paramount importance.

Recording in science

Within the science investigative cycle the recording and communicating of results is a very important aspect. Children should be aware of the most useful types of records and the relative merits of using diagrams, tables, bar charts, photos, written accounts etc. As teachers, however, we should always check that what we ask the children to do and to record is relevant to the learning intentions for a particular lesson.

For example, if the children have planned their own experiments and controlled the variables writing up the method used may be appropriate. If though, the class has simply followed instructions it may be more valuable for the children to spend the available time for recording their observations, results and conclusions. In addition, if written records are requested, they should always be for a genuine purpose. Children should understand why they are recording and how the records will help their scientific understanding. Within science, recording of methods should provide sufficient details to allow experiments to be replicated and thus lead to similar results to those obtained previously.

Creative records

Although the more traditional recounts of investigations and written records may be necessary, and indeed appropriate, for a given activity, at other times more creative records may be beneficial. Records such as posters, leaflets, booklets, PowerPoint presentations and photos can provide valuable, scientific information whilst at the same time motivate and enthuse the children to want to investigate.

Making a model of an observed plant can reveal the children's knowledge and understanding of the parts and their purpose. As a child tries to make a flower that could turn towards the light or roots that could anchor the plant they are able to use technical language for a purpose and demonstrate understanding. Inventing an insect from a lump of play dough can reveal knowledge of adaptation and habitats.

In contrast, a worksheet can be so focused that a child is unable to show the full extent of their knowledge. A ten year old girl was recently asked in a written assessment to give two reasons for choosing plastic as the material to make a water bottle. She failed to write a response. When asked later, why she had not responded Rosie replied "I knew six reasons so I wasn't sure which ones were wanted."

Assessing science

In recent years there has been increasing discussion on what, when and how assessment should take place in school. Terms such as 'feed-forward and feedback'; 'formative and summative assessment'; 'assessment for learning (AFL) and assessment of learning (AOL)' and 'assessment of pupil performance (APP)' have all become commonly used phrases in school.

Essentially, assessment should be about finding out what children know, understand and can do, in order that they can be helped to progress and develop. Sadly, league tables and Standard Assessment Tests (SATs) have, at times, distorted the way assessment has been used with the result that the needs of the children have not always been kept at the centre of the assessment process.

Typical assessments within science have, in the past, used pencil and paper tests. Children are asked to tick responses, fill in gaps and label diagrams. They have tended to assess content and knowledge requiring the children to memorise key vocabulary. Unfortunately many children are unable through such tests to show the real depth of their scientific understanding. In particular, their ability to plan and carry out investigations has often been underestimated with tests focusing mainly on content. Investigational questions have tended to consider the reading of data from graphs and tables, and the control of variables. Such questions seem, at times, to be a 'token gesture'.

Whilst teachers must fit in with school and national guidelines for assessment procedures, the golden rule for teacher assessments within science should be to keep them manageable and, most importantly, useful. Useful records will show what a child knows and where they can be developed next. They will not necessarily show everything a child knows or can do but should be an accurate reflection of the child.

Assessment might involve observations of the children at work; discussions and questioning; and consideration of products such as drawings, models and written work. By using a variety of approaches children will have the maximum opportunity to achieve. It must also be recognised that assessments that are based on written evidence may not always reflect what a child knows. An example of this is a Year 2 child who was asked to draw what she noticed when observing a pencil in a beaker of water. This is what she drew.
It appears that Connie has failed to notice that the pencil seems to bend when placed in a glass of water. Yet when asked what she noticed about the pencil in water she said, "It looked funny, sort of bent." When asked why she had drawn the pencil straight and not as she had seen it Connie replied, "Because that's the way the pencil is, it's straight. It looks bent but that's just pretend. Really the pencil is straight. Pencils don't bend when they're left in water – at least I don't think they do. Can we see?" This conversation is evidence of a child with good observational skills and understanding of refraction. The picture alone, however, would not have assessed Connie's understanding or observational skills.

A popular assessment tool often used within science is that of 'concept maps'. A concept map can reflect a child's understanding for a topic both before it starts and after its completion. Children are asked to link a set of words or pictures with arrows and words to show their understanding of relationships.

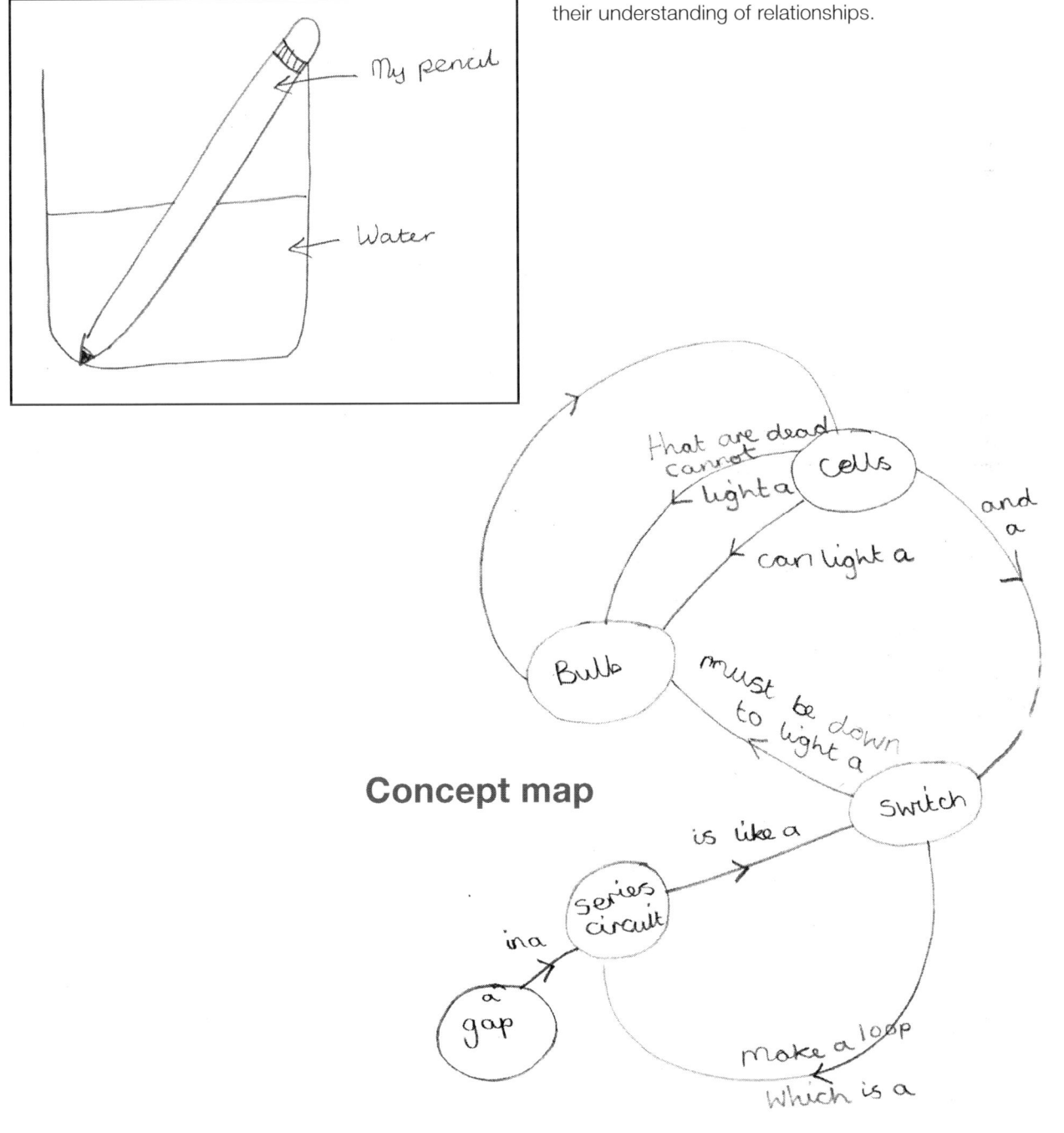

Concept map

Using ICT

ICT is being increasingly used within all areas of the primary school curriculum. ICT includes not only computers, but also a variety of resources such as sensors to measure light, sound and heat; digital cameras and microscopes; electronic timers and audio cassette recorders. For researching topics and ideas, and developing understanding of areas such as the Earth in space and the functions of organs within the human body, the use of the internet and CD ROMs can be invaluable. Interactive whiteboards are extremely useful when used in plenaries to gather results from a class and display them instantly in graphs and/or charts. It is though, important to remember that computers for science should be seen as a valuable resource. They must not replace activities that could readily be done through hands-on, practical activity. For example, useful revision might involve a whiteboard activity dragging words to label a picture of a plant. This should not though replace the direct experience of using plants. Thus, when planning, teachers must evaluate how the use of ICT not only matches the conceptual learning intentions for the lesson, but also develops children's understanding of scientific investigation.

Using cross-curricular links

Science has much to offer many areas within the primary curriculum, and vice-versa. The skills of observation and measuring are also used within design and technology and art, whilst knowledge of graphs and tables is helpful in maths and geography. Many scientific concepts are relevant for other curriculum areas. Understanding of how the body works relates to PE; facts about making and changing sounds reinforces ideas experienced in music; consideration of environmental change and recycling is relevant in science and geography and knowledge of materials is useful in art and DT. Many other examples of cross-curricular links are equally valuable. Encouraging the children to make links between subjects can give them a deeper level of understanding and also reinforce the value of what they do. For teachers, using cross-curricular links can make better use of the time available for teaching. Teaching children how to use glossaries or an index within non-fiction texts, for instance, could happen within English or a subject like science, geography or history. What is taught within any one of these areas will have value for them all. The Early Years Foundation Stage recognises the value of fostering links through its use of areas of learning such as Knowledge and Understanding of the World. This approach is equally valuable throughout the primary years.

Displays

Displays within science essentially fall into three categories: for information, for recording results and

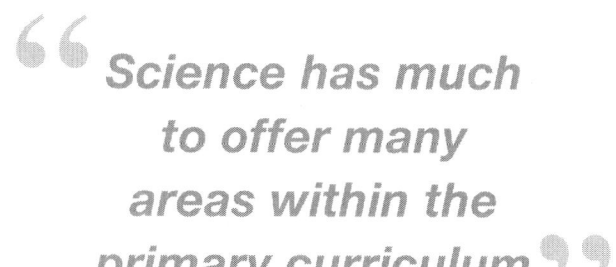

> Science has much to offer many areas within the primary curriculum

observations, and to celebrate achievements. A good way to start a topic is to have a display that introduces the children to key ideas and vocabulary. This display should be interactive with questions to encourage the children to search the display; items that the children can handle and a limited number of books that can be changed for others as the topic progresses. For example a topic on forces might be stimulated with a notice stating 'a force is a push or a pull' and photos of things that involve forces.

A table could be set out with safe toys that demonstrate movement, and question cards that ask the children how the toys start to move and whether any involve magnets. Books, both fiction and non-fiction, giving information on forces or showing pictures of pushes and pulls would also be useful. Time would need to be made available for the children to be able to interact with the display. If used appropriately children would then come to their science lessons with awareness of forces in action and an understanding of the key words 'push' and 'pull'.

Displays are often used to record observations and measurements over a period of time. Examples of this include having a pond background where children can add drawings/collages of frogspawn, tadpoles and frogs that have been observed. The pictures would be added each time a change was noted in the cycle such as the hatching of the tadpoles or the development of legs. Each picture would need a label with a date. As an alternative the changes in the cycle could be represented with dated pictures hung from a suspended hoop. Heights of sunflowers being observed from seed to flowering could be recorded each week with a strip of paper. The strips could then be arranged on a board to give a block graph. As with all graphs, the display would need a title and labels for the axes.

Displays for celebrations and achievements within science should include any work of which the children and teachers are proud. The pride might be for a result, a method, or the way that observations are recorded. What matters for these types of display is that all the children over the course of the year have the opportunity to contribute and that the emphasis is on science. In addition, the displays should be open to an audience wider than the class such as parents and children in other year groups.

Catering for Individual Needs

All lessons should be planned to be appropriate to meet the individual needs of the children. Sometimes this may involve modifying an experiment or changing a method for recording results. Care should be taken to match lessons to children's scientific understanding. Some schools place children in ability groups for English and mathematics and then they use the same groupings for science. Whilst in some cases this might be appropriate, for others this may limit what a child has the opportunity to learn. Being good at English or mathematics will not necessarily indicate that a child will excel in science. Equally, being weak at the subjects may not mean the child will be poor in science.

The practical nature of science can prove hard for children with weak fine motor skills. One way for teachers to ensure that they plan appropriate practical activities for such children is for them to wear thick, woollen, gloves when trialing the experiments. If the activity can be carried out in the gloves, weak fine motor skills should not be an issue.

Sensitivity to children's individual circumstances should always be taken into account at the planning stage for a topic. For example, a request to bring in baby clothes or photos for a project on the human life cycle may be inappropriate for children who do not live with their birth family. Class surveys of physical differences can be a source of embarrassment for some children. Whilst they may not mind having the widest hand span they may not want to be weighed or have their height measured.

Awareness of physical problems such as colour blindness or impairments to hearing and vision can be crucial for topics on sound, sight and colour. Children diagnosed with 'weak auditory processing' or 'weak working memories' may have difficulty remembering more than two instructions or copying information from a board. For such children a pictorial prompt sheet for an experiment or a vocabulary check list that replaces the need to copy from a whiteboard can be extremely beneficial.

Within any class there will be a wide range of levels of ability for understanding concepts. Care should be taken when offering extension activities that they do extend. Extension is not simply a matter of providing 'more of the same' or just expecting the children to write longer reports. It is about challenging the children to deepen their scientific understanding. Experiments, for example, could involve a greater number of variables. Measurements might be taken with more sensitive equipment or using more refined scales. Essentially the important thing to remember when planning for science is to make it stimulating, available and accessible to all children.

Planning to teach Science in the Primary Classroom

Section 2

Developing skills

Section 1 described how planning for science must consider both the skills and the concepts. Often the same activity can be carried out with a different age of class but for different learning intentions. Thus, it is vital for both the teacher and the children to consider what the activity intends to promote. For example, in Year 1 children might be given a selection of objects to sort according to whether they might float or sink and then be asked to test their predictions. In Year 6 the same activity might take place but the children would be expected to consider the forces involved and the concept of balanced and unbalanced. Children within Key Stage 1 might collaborate with an adult to list factors that affect the germination of cress seeds. At Key Stage 2 children, hopefully, could list and control the variables before planning and carrying out their investigation.

Section 2 gives details of activities, for teachers to select the ones that they feel would match the knowledge and understanding they wish their pupils to develop. Skills are not given for each activity because these will depend on the year group, the way the topic is introduced and the degree to which the children plan and carry out the activity and evaluate their findings.

In recent years there has been discussion on content overload and concern for the limited amount of practical investigation that children, particularly in Key Stage 2, have been able to do. There are, however, a number of key points to remember when planning science lessons for children. Firstly, although the National Curriculum states what children have to know it does not specify the methods for teaching science or what the children should actually do. As a result, it is up to schools and teachers to ensure that what they provide for children balances content and practical activity. Issues of content overload have been related to the use of Standard Assessment Tests (SATs).

Activity Levels

A number of published science schemes exist that specify an activity is suitable for a particular year group. Unfortunately such schemes do not account for the individual circumstances of a school or class, and can lead to inappropriate labelling of activities as appropriate or otherwise. To avoid this, the majority of activities within this book have not been allocated to a particular key stage. This is because some of the learning intentions within the National Curriculum for Key Stage 1 are similar to ones given for Key Stage 2 but expressed in simpler terms. Where intentions only appear in Key Stage 2, such as for micro-organisms, the Learning Intentions have been marked with the symbol *. It is though important that schools plan for progression. Care should be taken, if repeating activities in subsequent years, that children continue to be engaged and recognise the additional understanding that they have gained.

Safety

Although all the activities outlined within this book have been trialled with children aged five to eleven years, teachers should, in addition to the safety points noted in Section 1, consider the following when allowing children to work with animals and/or plants:

Safety when working with plants

Teach children to treat all plants and fungi as hazards until it is known that they are safe. In Great Britain it is illegal to dig up wild plants or to pick some wild flowers. In general it is acceptable to allow children to pick safe, common weeds. It must though be remembered that some plants contain toxic chemicals and as a result are poisonous. Poisonous plants include ones such as holly, laburnum, privet, ragwort, yew, white bryony, black nightshade and woody nightshade. Plants also can irritate the skin or cause dermatitis. Examples of these are stinging nettles, giant hogweed and some bulbs of the lily family.

When working with plants children should be taught:
- never to taste any part unless it is certain that it is safe to do so;
- to avoid touching eyes;
- to wash hands after touching plants or seeds.

Safety when pond dipping

Avoid areas with difficult or steep access. Weil's disease is a rare bacterial disease that can cause influenza like symptoms. It can be caught from water polluted by rats. Thus pond dipping should not take place from water where there is waste human food as this encourages rats to gather.

When pond dipping children should be taught:
- to avoid splashes that cause water to enter the eyes, nose or throat;
- to cover cuts and abrasions with waterproof plasters;
- to wash hands and other areas that have come into contact with the water (e.g. knees).

Activities to teach Life and Living Things at KS1/2

Life processes

Learning intentions
- Pupils will understand the difference between things that are living and things that have never been alive.
- Pupils will know that the life processes common to plants include growth, nutrition and reproduction.
- Pupils will be able relate life processes to animals and plants found in the local environment.

Activities
- Compare a doll or teddy with a human. List the similarities and the differences. How do the children know that the teddy/doll is not living?

- Tell the children an alien has arrived on the Earth. He has been sent to take three living things back to his planet but does not know the difference between what is living and what is not.

  Ask the class to help him by making a list of characteristics for a living thing. (Note: Characteristics for things to be classified as living include an ability to: move, reproduce, be sensitive, take up nutrition, excrete, respire, and grow.)

  Use the lists to sort the pictures in Copy Master 7 into 'living' and 'has never been alive'. As a class, tell the alien which three things to take back and explain what he will need to do to keep them alive.

- Take the children on a walk around the school. Identify living things.

- Take the children on a safe walk around the school grounds. Identify places where plants are growing and mark them on a plan. Inside discuss how the plants' needs are met by their habitats.
- Use the internet to research the life processes for a plant such as an apple tree.

Humans and other animals
Learning intention
- Pupils will be able to recognise and compare the main external parts of the bodies of humans and other animals.

Activities
- Draw round a child wearing trousers. Label as many body parts as possible.

- Enjoy making hand and footprints. Cut them out and compare the similarities and differences.

- Use a digital camera to take photos of children. Ask each child to make a paper plate mask to represent their own face. Compare the similarities and differences.

- Play 'Simon says' using as many body part words as possible. Invite children to lead the game.

- Make imaginary animals. Encourage the children to use body part words to describe their animals. Use the pictures to play 'I spy an animal that has ...'

- Set out activities such as building towers of bricks, placing pegs in or out of a pegboard, spooning marbles through a hole in a margarine tub, removing pincer clothes pegs from a line using one hand and using chop sticks to stack sugar cubes. Compare the way that children use their hands. Use ICT to record what each hand can do.

Planning to teach Science in the Primary Classroom

Senses
Learning intention
- Pupils will know about the senses that enable humans and other animals to be aware of the world around them.

Activities
- Having first checked for potential food allergies, enjoy carrying out sense testing using foods. Which foods can be identified by smell? Can foods be identified by taste? If foods have been pureed can they be recognised or does the texture matter?

- Use ICT and books to research the similarities and differences in the eyes and ears of humans and other animals. Encourage the children to consider why particular senses are important for a specific animal and how animals' senses have adapted for their surroundings.

- Carry out hearing tests. Sit the class in a large circle around a child wearing a blindfold. Investigate whether the blindfolded child can identify where sounds are being made. Repeat the experiment with a child also wearing headphones and a hat that covers the ears. If hearing is less good, relate this to road safety and the need to listen.

Teeth
Learning intention
- Pupils will know about the functions and care of teeth.

Activities
- Invite a dental hygienist/dentist to talk to the class about teeth. Following the visit make posters or non-fiction books to describe the care and functions of teeth.

- Use secondary sources to research the function of canine, molar and incisor teeth. Provide raw carrots for the children to eat. Encourage the children to analyse how they use their teeth.

- Collect packaging from tooth brushes, dental floss and toothpaste. Investigate how the products claim to protect teeth.

Exercise and healthy diets
Learning intentions
- Pupils will know that humans and other animals need food and water to stay alive.
- Pupils will know that taking exercise and eating the right types and amounts of food help humans to keep healthy.

Activities
- Give each child Copy Master 9 which shows the proportions of foods that should be eaten to make a balanced diet. Ask them to either stick on pictures of food cut from magazines or draw foods to show a healthy, balanced lunch. Older children should know that protein is needed for growth and repair; carbohydrates are needed for energy, and fats are needed for healthy skin and stored energy. Talk about the importance of drinking water.

- Collect clean food packets. Make a large collage of the packets. Use the display to analyse the nutritional content. Compare the energy, fat and carbohydrate contents for 100g of given foods. Which foods provide minerals and vitamins? Talk about what is meant by 'the Recommended Daily Allowance' values given on foods such as boxes of cereal.

- Investigate the fat content in a variety of foods by pressing equal sized pieces of food such as crisps, croissant, chocolate, cake and pastry on a clean piece of paper. Remove the food and examine the paper for marks. Translucent marks that do not disappear on drying indicate fat. Wet patches that disappear on drying suggest the presence of water.

- Make a class display to show all the types of exercise that children do in a week. Talk about how the exercise helps people to be healthy. Which parts of the body are helped by different types of exercise? (The following table shows some examples of popular forms of exercise and the extent to which they build strength, suppleness and stamina.) Remember to include exercise such as walking up stairs, carrying shopping, and cleaning, which the children may not associate with the term 'exercise'.

Exercise	Stamina	Strength	Suppleness
Cycling	***	**	*
Football	**	**	**
Gymnastics	*	**	***
Jogging	***	*	*
Swimming	***	***	***
Trampolining	***	***	***

- During a PE lesson annotate a diagram of the human body to show safe ways to exercise different parts of the body. Copy Master 4 could be used.

Hearts

Learning intentions
- Pupils will know that the heart acts as a pump to circulate the blood through vessels around the body, including through the lungs.
- Pupils will know about the effect of exercise and rest on pulse rate.

Activities
- Measure the pulse rate for 30 seconds before and after carrying out exercises such as running on the spot or skipping. Check the children are aware that a pulse beats each time the heart beats. Explain that when we exercise our muscles require more oxygen and therefore the pulse/heart rate quickens.

- Use ICT and secondary sources to explain how the heart works.

Skeletons

Learning intention
- Pupils will know that humans and some other animals have skeletons and muscles to support and protect their bodies and to help them to move.

Activities
- Use the skeleton (Copy Master 4) to analyse how joints work. Mark on the sheet ball and socket joints and hinge joints. Discuss how muscles work in pairs.

- Give pairs or small groups of children an A5 sized outline of a human cut from fabric. Challenge the children to get the body to stand up. Provide straws, pipe-cleaners, card etc for the children to make skeletons for their bodies. Discuss how skeletons provide support.

- Research skulls on the internet. Talk about the importance of cycle helmets for protecting skulls and brains.

- Tell children that muscles work in pairs and that to move a bone a muscle must contract/shorten. Encourage them to feel the muscles in the upper arm as the arm is bent and straightened. Push a block of dough or Plasticine to demonstrate that as muscles contract they get fatter.

- Prepare a collection of sterile meat bones by boiling the bones. Ask the children to research the bones using books and the internet. Talk about the different functions of specific bones. Sketch the bones with white crayons on black paper.

Life cycles

Learning intentions
- Pupils will know about the main stages of the human life cycle.
- Pupils will know that humans and other animals can produce offspring and that these offspring grow into adults.
- Pupils will know how to treat animals with care and sensitivity.

Activities
- Make a time line, using pictures, to show the human lifecycle.

- Observe and record the changes for frogspawn developing into frogs, eggs hatching to be chicks or caterpillars to butterflies.

- Make a time line, mobile or concertina book to show the lifecycle for an observed animal.

Drugs

Learning intentions
- Pupils will know about the role of drugs as medicines.
- Pupils will know about the effects on the human body of tobacco, alcohol and other drugs, and how these relate to their personal health.

Activities
- Ask the children what they think is meant by the word 'drugs'. Make a collection of packets/labels from coffee, wine, cigarettes, over-the-counter cough mixtures, prescription drugs, glue, coke, fizzy fruit drinks. Ask the children to select the ones that they feel are drugs. Discuss the children's choices and explain that drugs include nicotine, caffeine, various solvents and alcohol in addition to the prescribed and shop bought drugs.

- Invite a child who uses an asthma inhaler or insulin pen to explain their use. Emphasise that prescribed drugs are only for the person for whom they have been prescribed.

Green plants

Learning intentions
- Pupils will recognise that plants need light and water to grow.
- Pupils will understand the effect of light, air, water and temperature on plant growth.
- Pupils will recognise and name the leaf, flower, stem and root of flowering plants.
- Pupils will understand the role of the leaf in producing new material for growth.

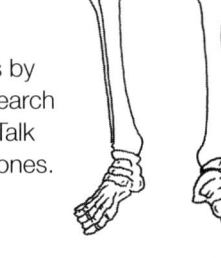

- Pupils will know that the root anchors the plant, and that water and minerals are taken in through the root and transported through the stem to other parts of the plant.
- Pupils will know that seeds grow into flowering plants.
- Pupils will know about the parts of the flower [for example, stigma, stamen, petal, sepal] and their role in the life cycle of flowering plants, including pollination, seed formation, seed dispersal and germination.

Activities

- Look closely for seeds in fruits such as peppers, apples, cucumbers and watermelon. Where are the seeds? Do all fruits contain seeds? Invite each child to select a fruit to draw. Encourage them to match the pastel/chalk colours and to mix different colours by rubbing with a cotton wool ball. Note: When finished the pastel/chalk pictures can be 'fixed' with hair spray by an adult, in a well ventilated area.

- Make a collection of different types of apple. Compare their colours, scents and sizes. Cut the apples and count how many pips are in each apple. Examine the pips with a magnifier and compare them. Have any split? Plant the pips and over the weeks observe whether any germinate.

- Grow 'grassy hair' by placing a small handful of grass seed in the toes of an ankle sock sized piece cut from no longer needed nylon tights. Fill the rest of the foot with sawdust and knot the ankle tightly. Squash the bundle into a head shape and use a permanent pen to draw on face features. Soak the head and leave it to stand in a plastic pot. Each day check that the head is still damp and wait for the 'hair' to grow.

- Roll blotting paper into a cylinder shape and place it in a clear plastic beaker touching the sides. Place two beans between the blotting paper and beaker about one third of the way down from the beaker top. Pour water into the beakers to a depth of about 4cm. Leave the beakers where they can be viewed easily without being knocked. Each day check to see whether the seeds have germinated and observe how they develop.

- As a class list all the variables that could affect seed germination and plant growth such as water, light, darkness and temperature. Place scrunched up paper towel in the bottom of several plastic beakers and equal quantities of cress seed. Place two beakers in each of a variety of areas. Water one beaker in each area. Observe the plants each day and record what happens.

- Use Copy Master 15 to make a 'Germinating Seed Flick Book'.

- Talk about plants that can be eaten and which parts. Grow plants that can be eaten.

- Sort leaves according to characteristics such as shape, surface texture, colour and edge. Research the purpose of pores and veins. Explore which leaves can be used to make prints. Which leaves show the most veins?

- Investigate whether plants can survive without leaves. Carry out observations of two similar plants with and without leaves. Record what happens with a digital camera.

- Observe and draw a variety of roots. Record the roots using white crayons on black paper.

Variation and classification
Learning intentions

- Pupils will be able to group living things according to observable similarities and differences.
- Pupils will make and use keys.
- Pupils will know how locally occurring animals and plants can be identified and assigned to groups.

Activities

- Use Copy Masters 10, 11 and 12 to identify plants and minibeasts found around the school.

- As a class make a branching key to distinguish four children.

- Make close observations of three insects, leaves or plants in the local environment. Make branching keys to sort the insects/plants.

- Talk about the different ways animals are sorted into groups. Discuss useful ways to sort animals.

Living things in their environment

Learning intentions
- Pupils will find out about the different kinds of plants and animals in the local environment.
- Pupils will identify similarities and differences between local environments and ways in which these affect animals and plants that are found there.
- Pupils will know how to care for the environment.
- Pupils will know about ways in which living things and the environment need protection.
- Pupils will know about the different plants and animals found in different habitats.
- Pupils will how animals and plants in two different habitats are suited to their environment.

Activities
- Investigate where minibeasts in the school grounds live. Complete Copy Master 8 to show where they are found. Are there any minibeasts not present that might have been expected? If so, what could be done to encourage their presence?

- Use an identification sheet to identify a range of minibeasts.

- Go on an 'insect's nature walk'. Ask the children to lay a 2 metre length of string on the ground in the shape of a letter such as C, S or W. Encourage the children to follow the string from the insect's point of view, examining the trail in detail. What plants would the insect pass? Do any of them have flowers? Will the insect meet any other creatures? Make a map to record the insect's journey.

- Make detailed drawings of two minibeasts on small pieces of paper.

- Make a key to distinguish four minibeasts or four plants.

- It is has been estimated that hedgerows contain over 600 plant species, 1500 species of insects, 65 species of birds and 20 species of mammals. As a class investigate how many different species of animals and plants can be found in a safe, local hedge.

- Outside, lay a hoop on a grassy area. Encourage the children to notice the variety of plants within the hoop. Are all the leaves and grasses the same green? Which plants are insects most attracted to?

- Observe how dandelion and sycamore seeds are dispersed by the wind. Discuss why dispersal is necessary. Back inside make paper versions (see Copy Master 13 for making models of sycamore seeds). Which 'paper seeds' (sycamores)/ tissue paper parachutes (dandelion seeds) fall the slowest. On a windy day explore which of the 'paper seeds' travel the furthest when dispersed by the wind. Ensure the testing is fair.

- Enjoy pond dipping in a safe area (e.g. school pond or at an environmental studies centre). Identify any creatures within a sample of pond water.

- Take samples from defined zones within the pond such as the edge, water surface, submerged weed, emergent weed and at different depths. Compare the samples to investigate whether some creatures prefer particular habitats.

- Make posters or leaflets for a 'Habitat Agency' to advertise habitats suited to particular animals.

- Make a habitat for a snail or woodlouse.

- Use sensors to record values for the humidity, light and temperature for different habitats.

- Use ICT to compare habitats around the world with the local environment.

Feeding relationships

Learning intentions
- Children will use food chains to show feeding relationships in a habitat.
- Children will know that nearly all food chains start with a green plant.

Activities
- As a class make food chains for a child and a garden bird. Explain that the arrow represents the flow of energy. Help children to realise that most food chains start with green plants.

- Carry out class surveys in the local environment to discover what a range of animals, including birds and insects, eat. Use the class data to make food chains. Compare the chains.

- Make food chains for animals found in a pond and a hedge. Compare the food chains for the two habitats, noting the similarities and the differences.

- Challenge the children to make the longest, possible food chain.

- Use the internet to research food chains that do not start with a green plant. (Note: One example food chain uses bacteria that live in darkness near the hydrothermal vents of the Pacific Ocean. They take in simple chemicals to transform into complex food materials. Deep sea animals eat the bacteria.)

Micro-organisms

Learning intention

- Children will know that that micro-organisms are living organisms that are often too small to be seen, and that they may be beneficial [for example, in the breakdown of waste, in making bread] or harmful [for example, in causing disease, in causing food to go mouldy].

Activities

- Talk about germs and how they can lead to illness. Explain that 'germ' is an everyday word used to describe micro-organisms that cause disease. Use secondary sources to research ways to inhibit the spreading of germs.

- Look at samples of mouldy fruit, bread and cheese in sealed containers. Use magnifiers to observe the mouldy foods and make close observational drawings. (SAFETY: The containers should be disposed of without being opened.)

- Introduce children to live yeast as a micro-organism. Discuss what yeast needs to live. Make bread with and without yeast. Compare the differences.

- Use the internet to research the role of micro-organisms in causing food poisoning.

Activities to teach Materials and their properties

Grouping and classifying materials

Learning intentions

- Pupils will use their senses to explore and recognise the similarities and differences between materials.
- They will sort objects into groups on the basis of simple material properties.
- They will find out about the uses of a variety of materials and how these are chosen for specific uses on the basis of their simple properties.
- They will recognise and name common types of material and recognise that some of them are found naturally.

Activities

- Sort bins of clean rubbish by material. Discuss which ones can be recycled.

- Sort objects according to the materials from which they were made. Discuss why specific materials are chosen for particular objects.

- Play the 'Yes/No Game' in which a chosen object is identified by questions relating to the material(s) from which it is made. E.g. Is it soft? Is it made of metal? Does it contain a gas?

- Describe the appearance and textures of different types of paper (e.g. Kitchen towel, tissue paper, writing paper, sugar paper, newsprint, wrapping paper). Discuss the properties needed for each type of paper. Could one paper be used for all the required functions?

- Sort materials according to a given criteria such as shiny or 'visible at night'. Use the selected materials for a task such as 'Make a shiny collage' or make a collage of a dress that would help Cinderella to be visible walking home after the ball'.

- Go for a walk around the school. Identify the materials used for furniture, buildings and flooring. Identify the natural materials.

- Use labels to sort clothes according to the fabrics from which they are made. Compare the texture and appearance (use a magnifier or digital microscope). Use books or the internet to discover which fabrics are natural (e.g. cotton, wool, silk) and which ones are man-made (e.g. acrylic, polyester). Make a fact file of fabrics where each child contributes one page. Stick on samples of fabric.

- Investigate which materials are absorbent/ waterproof/ magnetic/ transparent/ translucent/ opaque/ conduct electricity … Can wax crayons be used to make card waterproof?

- Investigate the best material for a boat sail/ parachute/carrier bag/tights.

- Classify a range of familiar materials, at room temperature, as gas, liquid or solid.

- Compare the viscosity of common, safe liquids (e.g. golden syrup, soup, honey) by observing teaspoons of each moving down a sloping, flat plastic tray. What happens if the tray is warm?

- Compare sandcastles made from wet and dry sand.

Keeping warm

Learning intention

- Pupils will know that some materials are better thermal insulators than others.

Activities

- Make a list of ways to keep food cool such as freezer bags and flasks. Analyse the materials that are used.

- Investigate ways to prevent ice cubes from melting. Provide a range of materials for the children to debate whether they would be good thermal insulators. Give each child their own ice cube to wrap wit their chosen insulation. See how effective it has been after a given period of time. Talk about ways to make the investigation fair.

- Pick out clothing that would be good to wear on a cold winter's day. Relate the clothing to thermal insulation.

- Place a variety of similar sized spoons made from a variety of materials (e.g. metal, wood, plastic) in a beaker of warm water. Investigate which is the best conductor of heat. Explain that good thermal insulators are poor conductors of heat.

Rocks and soils
Learning intention

- Pupils will describe and group rocks and soils on the basis of their characteristics, including appearance, texture and permeability.

Activities

- Observe samples of rocks such as granite, slate and marble. Talk about the properties of different types of rock and their uses. Explain that rocks are natural but that many building materials, such as bricks, are not.

- Sort rocks into groups according to observable features. Check that the children understand that pebbles and stones are just pieces of rock.

- Compare the permeability for a variety of rocks by observing what happens when small amounts of water are placed on the surface.

- Compare a variety of samples of soil. Provide sieves and magnifiers. (SAFETY: Ensure the samples have been collected from safe areas that are not contaminated by dog faeces, broken glass etc. Hands must be washed after the soils have been observed.)

- Test how quickly water seeps through sandy soil and clay-based soil. Place equal volumes in two identical plastic plant pots that have small holes in their bases. Pour in identical amounts of water and observe how quickly water starts to come through. Are equal quantities of water collected?

Solids, liquids and gases
Learning intention

- Pupils will recognise differences between solids, liquids and gases, in terms of ease of flow and maintenance of shape and volume.

Activities

- Use Copy Master 16 to introduce solids, liquids and gases. Ask the children to classify each of the listed materials as a gas, liquid or solid at room temperature and to give reasons for their choices.

- Make and investigate 'corn flour gloop' by mixing corn flour with water, in a large bowl (e.g. washing up bowl), to form a thick consistency. Debate whether it is a solid or liquid. (Note: Corn flour gloop if picked up with a hand will flow through the fingers like a liquid. If squeezed it appears hard and like a solid.)

Changing materials
Learning intentions

- Pupils will know that the shapes of objects made from some materials can be changed by some processes, including squashing, bending, twisting and stretching.
- They will know that some everyday materials change when they are heated or cooled. *They will describe the changes.
- They will know about reversible changes, including dissolving, melting, boiling, condensing, freezing and evaporating.

Activities

- Make play-dough by mixing 1 cup salt, 2 cups flour and approximately 1 cup water. Explore its properties. Investigate how the shape of a ball of dough can be changed by stretching, rolling, twisting etc.

- Investigate what happens when changes are made to the play-dough recipe. Possible ones include: adding oil; adding food colouring; mixing dough of two different colours; using half the quantity of flour; using different types of flour; using twice as much water.

- Recycle paper.
  1. Tear about 8 pages of a broadsheet newspaper into small pieces and place in a large container.
  2. Add 4 cups of water. (More may be needed – depends on how absorbent the paper is.) Pulp the paper by pulling it apart in the water.
  3. Drain the pulp. Spread it out on plastic lids, press firmly and leave it to dry in a sunny area.
  4. Each day examine the pulp as it dries to form a rough cardboard.
  5. Compare the recycled paper with newspaper.

6. Investigate recycling of other types of paper.
   Note: This activity will cause hands/containers to be stained. If desired plastic gloves can be worn for the pulping activity.

- Fill a balloon, plastic glove or plastic tub with water and freeze it. Compare frozen and liquid water. Observe the 'iceberg' melting. (If it snows, place a tub of clean snow in a freezer. Bring it out on a sunny day – it amazes children to see snow in the summer!)

- Investigate whether different types of chocolate held in a hand start to melt at the same time.

- Compare materials such as butter, margarine and cheeses when floated on a plastic tray in a bowl of warm water.

Learning intention

- Pupils will describe changes that occur when materials are mixed [for example, adding salt to water]

Activities

- Make a variety of types of icing. What happens to the sugar? Compare 'set' and liquid icing.

- On a calm day investigate blowing bubbles, outside, using a variety of blowers and mixtures, made by the children. What effect does adding glycerine to the mixture have? How much water can be added before the solution is too weak for bubbles to form?

Temperature
Learning intention

- Pupils will know that temperature is a measure of how hot or cold things are.

Activities

- For a week record the temperature at mid-day. Compare the temperatures with ones recorded on the internet or in a newspaper.

- Measure the temperature of a warm cup of water as it cools. Plot a graph to show how the temperature varies over time.

- Compare by touch the temperature of warm tap water, cold water and water from a fridge. Help the children to realise that hot and cold are comparative terms.

- Enjoy baking. Help the children to be aware of the temperature setting for the cooker and to realise how long it takes for the cooked items to cool down. (For children with food allergies an alternative is to use modelling dough that needs to be cooked.)

Non-reversible changes
Learning intentions

- Pupils will know that non-reversible changes [for example, vinegar reacting with bicarbonate of soda, plaster of Paris with water] result in the formation of new materials that may be useful.
- Pupils will know that burning materials [for example, wood, wax, natural gas] results in the formation of new materials and that this change is not usually reversible.

Activities

- Explore changes that occur when 'cooking' food such as bread, pizzas, pastry, biscuits, cakes, peppermint creams, 'chocolate crispies' or making jelly, porridge or mousse.

- Press shells into blocks of play dough or damp, firm sand in plastic beakers to make moulds. Encourage the children to observe as adults pour in plaster of Paris. When set closely observe the models, compare them with the original shells and talk about the non-reversible change that has taken place. (SAFETY: When mixing plaster of Paris with water heat will be produced. Children should not touch.)

- Mix a sample of bicarbonate of soda with vinegar. Make a time line to show the stages in the reaction and the time taken for the reaction to stop.

- On the internet research uses of bicarbonate of soda and plaster of Paris.

- Demonstrate what happens when postage stamp sized pieces of a range of safe materials (e.g. paper) are burnt over a night light in a metal tray. Discuss how the burning leads to the formation of new materials and that the changes cannot be reversed. (SAFETY: Do not burn PVC or other plastics. Follow school/area guidelines and carry out a full risk assessment for the activity.)

- Explain that burning can lead to the formation of harmful substances. Carry out research into the hazard labels used on clothing and furniture.

Separating mixtures of materials
Learning intentions

- Pupils will know how to separate solid particles of different sizes by sieving [for example, those in soil].
- They will know that some solids [for example, salt, sugar] dissolve in water to give solutions but some [for example, sand, chalk] do not.
- They will know how to separate insoluble solids from liquids by filtering.
- They will know how to recover dissolved solids by

evaporating the liquid from the solution.
- Pupils will use knowledge of solids, liquids and gases to decide how mixtures might be separated.

Activities
- Investigate ways to separate solid materials e.g. sand and dried peas by sieving, using a magnet to remove paperclips from rice …

- Use a magnifying glass to compare a fine sieve and a piece of filter paper. List their differences and similarities. Use a funnel and filter paper to separate sand from sand and water. Discuss ways that materials are separated around the home e.g. a tea bag, coffee filter papers, vacuum cleaner filters …

- Compare what happens when salt, sugar, powder paint, coffee, tea leaves, sand, flour, custard powder … are added to water. Establish understanding of the terms dissolving, solution, mixture, insoluble, soluble and saturated.

- Dissolve sugar or salt in water. Leave it in a shallow dish in a warm, safe area. Each day observe what happens as the water evaporates.

Activities to teach Energy, Movement and Forces

Electricity

Learning intention
- Pupils will know that some everyday appliances use electricity.

Activities
- Go for a walk around the classroom. Identify anything that uses electricity to work.

- Use a mail order catalogue to find pictures of things that use batteries and ones that run from mains electricity.

- Sort toys to find ones that run on electricity. Talk about ways to save energy. Are any of the toys solar powered?

Learning intention
- Pupils will know about simple series circuits involving batteries, wires, bulbs and other components such as buzzers and motors.

Activities
- Make simple circuits with a cell, a bulb and leads.

- Make a simple circuit with a cell, a bulb, leads and a gap. Investigate what can be used to fill the gap (e.g. a coin, a paper clip, a piece of foil) that will conduct electricity.

- Set challenges such as making a lift, using a motor and card circle as a colour wheel, drawing a street scene and using a lit bulb as the street light or sun to use components within a simple circuit.

Learning intention
- Pupils will know how a switch can be used to break a circuit.

Activities
- Make a simple circuit. Show the children that when there is a gap, the electricity cannot flow. Explain that a switch is a gap.

- Use switches within a simple circuit.

- Make a card and foil flap switch. Design new ways to make switches.

Card & flap switch

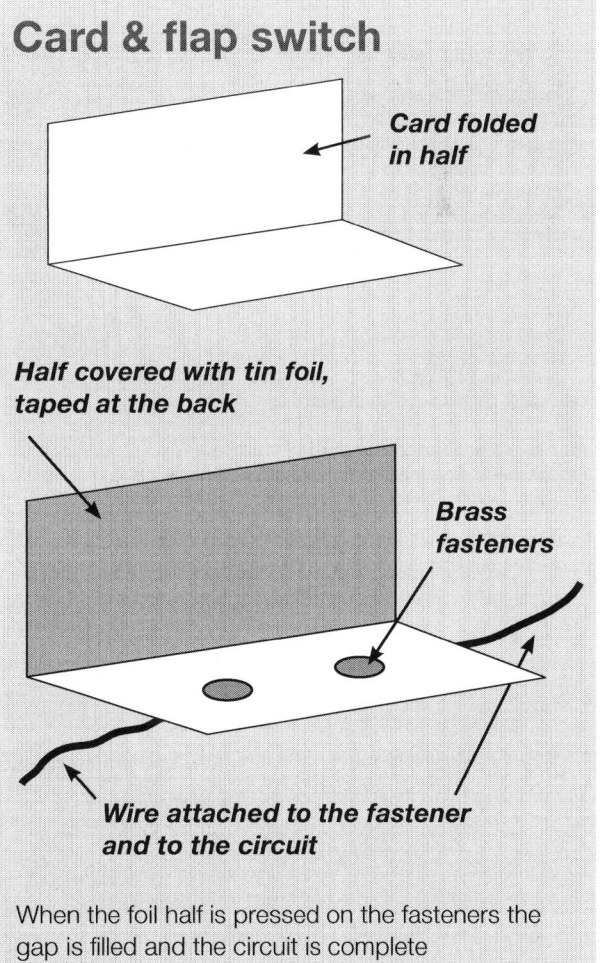

Card folded in half

Half covered with tin foil, taped at the back

Brass fasteners

Wire attached to the fastener and to the circuit

When the foil half is pressed on the fasteners the gap is filled and the circuit is complete

Learning intention
- Pupils will know how to represent series circuits by drawings and conventional symbols, and how to construct series circuits on the basis of drawings and diagrams using conventional symbols.

Activities
- Enjoy making simple circuits and recording them with drawings. Compare the drawings and the different ways that the children have represented bulbs, cells etc. Introduce conventional symbols. (Note: The glossary for Energy, Movement and Forces in Section 3 shows the conventional symbols used to represent an electrical circuit.)

- Provide paper or card symbols for electrical components (use Copy Master 17). Working in pairs, ask one child to lay out a simple circuit and their partner to make the circuit with components. (Note: Some blanks are given for children to draw in extra components they might need.)

- Make a quiz board. When complete, draw a diagram to show the circuit.

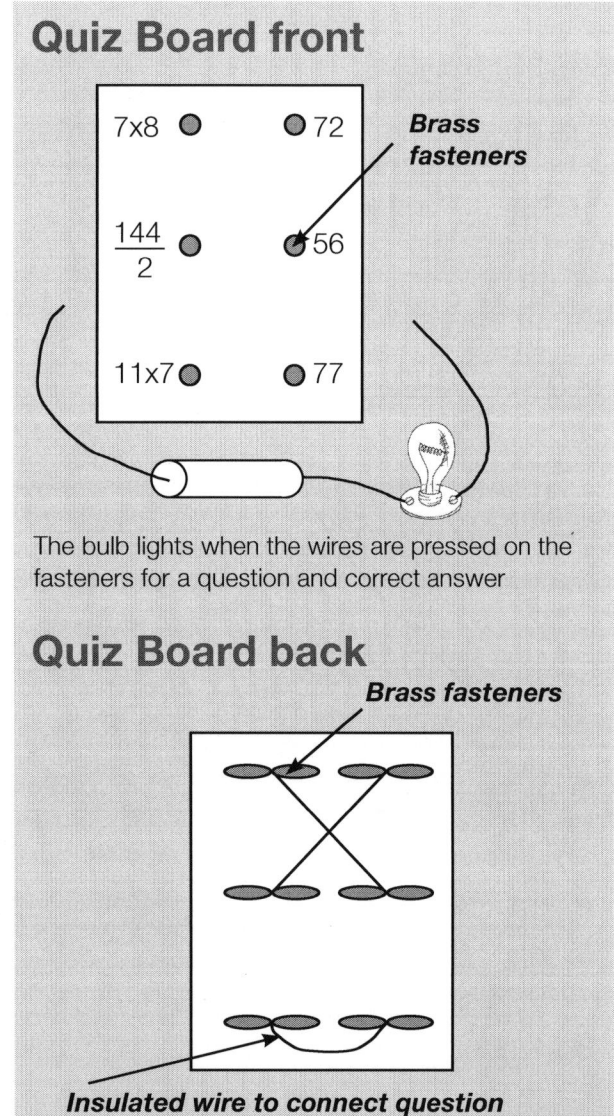

- Use stiff wire, a box and a series circuit to make a traditional 'loop and buzzer game'. Record the circuit.

- Draw a circuit diagram for a door bell, a burglar alarm or lighting for a dolls' house. If time allows, make the circuits.

Forces and motion
Learning intentions
- Pupils will find out about, and describe the movement of, familiar things.
- They will know that both pushes and pulls are examples of forces
- They will recognise that when things speed up, slow down or change direction, there is a cause [for example, a push or a pull].

Activities
- Write instruction labels using the words 'push' and 'pull' for anything that moves in the classroom (e.g. 'To open the door, push down on the handle and pull.' 'To turn the computer on push the power button.')

- Play with safe toys that move or have moving parts. Encourage the children to look for pushes and pulls, to know that a twist is a combination of a push and a pull and to describe the speeds and directions.

- Experiment with toppling dominoes. Where, should a domino be pushed to make it topple? What is the furthest distance apart that two dominoes can be placed for the first to knock over the second?

- Observe toy cars travelling down ramps (piece of thick card raised by books). Ask how to make the car go faster/slower/change direction.

- Outside investigate the movement of small kites, ribbons and bubbles. Describe how they move.

- Play parachute games. Describe the movement of the parachute.

Magnets
Learning intention
- Pupils will know about the forces of attraction and repulsion between magnets, and about the forces of attraction between magnets and magnetic materials.

Activities
- Play with magnetic games. Identify how the magnets are used and what is attracted/repelled.

- Investigate how strong a variety of magnets are by seeing through how many pieces of paper a paperclip can be attracted.

- Investigate how many paperclips a magnet can attract in a chain (Do not link the clips!)

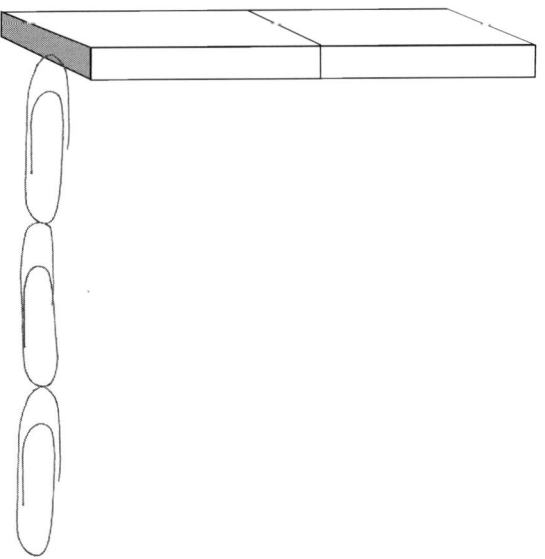

- Make a game that uses magnets.

- Sort materials according to whether they are magnetic or non-magnetic. Show how magnets can be used to sort materials when recycling cans.

Friction
Learning intention
- Pupils will understand that friction, including air resistance, is a force that slows moving objects and may prevent objects from starting to move.

Activities
- Investigate the way the size of canopy effects the way paper parachutes fall.

- Experience air resistance by playing parachute games.

- Try to move a large thick, hard-backed book by pushing with one finger. Show the children that if the book is placed on marbles the friction is reduced and the book can be moved easily.

- Make paper planes from pieces of A4 paper. Explore which ones fly the best. Which shape seems to cause the least air resistance? Why?

Forces in action and measuring forces
Learning intentions
- Pupils will know that when objects [for example, a spring, a table] are pushed or pulled, an opposing pull or push can be felt

- Pupils will know how to measure forces and identify the direction in which they act.

Activities
- Use a Newton balance (sometimes called a force meter) to weigh objects in Newtons (the unit of force).

- Use a Newton balance to weigh, in Newtons, objects that do not float. Then repeat the measurements but this time when the objects are suspended in water.

- Design and make a force meter using a yogurt pot, a ruler, weights and elastic bands. How accurate is it? (SAFETY: Place a box under the weights in case the band breaks. Be aware that snapped bands can cause painful 'flicks'.)

- Show children a heavy book squashing a spring; a paper clip hanging from a magnet and an object suspended on an elastic band. Talk about the forces acting on each object. Together draw diagrams to show the direction of the forces.

Light and dark
Learning intentions
- Pupils will identify different light sources, including the Sun.
- They will know that darkness is the absence of light.

Activities
- Ask the children to select light sources from a basket of objects such as a torch, a candle, a light bulb; pictures of the Moon, Sun and other stars, and items that are not sources of light. Then sort the light sources into primary sources, such as the Sun, that give light directly and then secondary ones, like the Moon, that reflect light.

- Identify all the light sources in a classroom and on a walk around the school.

- Make a light box from a box with a lid like a shoe box. The inside should be painted black or lined with black paper. At one end two small windows (eg squares of side 1cm) should be cut with a card curtain for one attached with a brass fastener.

Place a black toy car in the box. Investigate what can be seen when the curtain is shut and when it is open. Shine torch light through one of the windows. Does it affect what can be seen? Use cars in a variety of colours to investigate whether some colours are more visible than others.

Planning to teach Science in the Primary Classroom

Shadows

Learning intention
- The pupils will know that light cannot pass through some materials, and how this leads to the formation of shadows.

Activities
- Sort materials into translucent, transparent and opaque. Discuss where transparent materials and opaque ones might be useful. Select materials that could be used to make shadow puppets. Make the puppets. Explore how the sizes of shadows can be changed.

- On a sunny day, wearing appropriate sun protection, enjoy making shadows. Can children be identified from their shadows? What shapes can be made with hands?

Reflecting light and seeing

Learning intentions
- Pupils will know that light is reflected from surfaces [for example, mirrors, polished metals].
- Pupils will know that we see things only when light from them enters our eyes.

Activities
- Walk around the school to identify any surfaces that reflect light. Discuss where the reflecting is useful and when it might be irritating. Investigate ways to make mirrors.

- Play with periscopes and kaleidoscopes. Discuss how light is reflected in the mirrors.

- Place two mirrors at a right angle to each other. Place an object between the mirrors and see how many images can be seen in the mirrors. Vary the angle between the mirrors and see how the number of images changes.

- Use Copy Master 5 and the internet to research how we see. Draw ray diagrams to show how light is reflected from an object and enters the eye.

Making and detecting sounds

Learning intentions
- Pupils will know that there are many kinds of sound and sources of sound.
- Pupils will know that sounds are made when objects [for example, strings on musical instruments] vibrate but that vibrations are not always directly visible.

Activities
- Go on a sound walk to list sources of sound. Back in the classroom discuss which sounds were necessary and which ones might be classed as noise.

- Sort a collect of percussion instruments according to how they make the sound.

- Use a stringed instrument and a chime bar to show sounds made through vibrations. Show how the sound stops when the vibrations are stopped.

- Suspend a table tennis ball from a string. Hold a vibrating tuning fork close to the ball and show how the ball bounces as the fork vibrates. Fill a bowl with water and hold the vibrating fork on the surface. Observe how the water ripples.

Changing sounds and hearing

Learning intentions
- Pupils will know how to change the pitch and loudness of sounds produced by some vibrating objects (for example, a drum skin or a plucked string).
- They will know that vibrations from sound sources require a medium (for example, metal, wood, glass, air) through which to travel to the ear.
- Pupils will know that sounds travel away from sources, getting fainter as they do so, and that they are heard when they enter the ear.

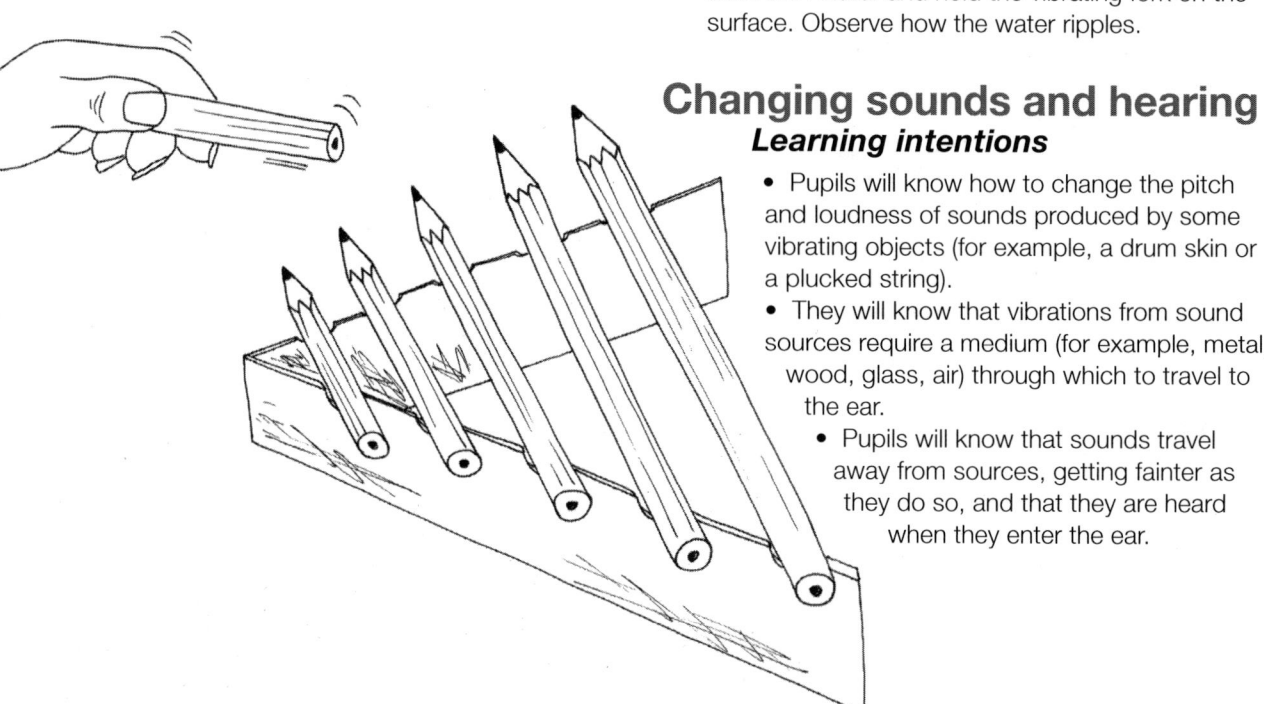

Activities

- Use milk bottles with varying amounts of water to play the first line of a simple tune such as 'I hear thunder' or 'Three blind mice'. Show how when tapping the bottles the bottle with the most water makes the lowest note (because the water is vibrating to cause the sound) whilst when blowing this bottle would cause the highest note (because the air vibrating causes the sound and in this case is the shortest column).

- Classify a variety of instruments according to how they make sounds. Discuss how the pitch and loudness can be changed.

- Make instruments to provide sound effects for a story. Use Copy Master 18 for ideas of simple ways to make instruments.

- Outside make a circle. Place one child at the centre with a quiet noise (e.g. small bell). Ask the children to walk slowly away from the child making the noise and to stop when the sound can no longer be heard. Inside, talk about the way the sound travelled and whether all children had the same level of hearing. Talk about the way the sound became fainter.

- Make string telephones from two plastic pots connected with string threaded through a hole at the centre of each base and knotted. Ask one child to whisper in one pot and another to listen through the other. Investigate the effect of changing the length and type of string and the size of pots. Does the string have to be taut?

The Sun, Earth and Moon
Learning intention
- Pupils will know that the Sun, Earth and Moon are approximately spherical.

Activity
- Challenge the children to find evidence to suggest that the Earth is approximately spherical. Help the children to use the internet and books. Look at a globe. Talk about watching ships appearing/ disappearing over the horizon. Having established that the Earth is spherical, gather further information about the Sun and Moon.

Periodic changes
Learning intentions
- Pupils will know how the position of the Sun appears to change during the day, and how shadows change as this happens.
- Pupils will know how day and night are related to the spin of the Earth on its own axis.
- Pupils will know that the Earth orbits the Sun once each year, and that the Moon takes approximately 28 days to orbit the Earth.

Activities
- Place a cone in the playground and record the position and size of its shadow at different times of day over a week.

- Use secondary sources to research how days and nights happen. Provide a large, a medium and a small ball. Challenge groups of children to use the balls to explain day and night.

- For a month ask the children to record the shape of the Moon either each morning or evening. Make a class display to show how the shape changes. Explain the reason for the change in terms of the Moon orbiting the Earth once every twenty eight days.

Planning to teach Science in the Primary Classroom

Background knowledge and glossaries for teachers

Section 3 provides some useful facts to support the development of teacher knowledge. It is hoped that the information may be of use when children ask knowledge related questions. In addition, glossaries explain some of the technical vocabulary.

Life processes and cells

- Living organisms exhibit seven life processes: movement, reproduction, sensitivity, nutrition, excretion, respiration, growth. To be alive, the organism must do all seven.
- There are three differences between plant and animal cells. All cells have a nucleus (to control what the cell does); cytoplasm (where chemical reactions take place) and a cell membrane (a thin skin that holds the cell together and controls what goes in and out). Only plant cells have: a cell wall (to give support); a vacuole (a large space filled with a weak solution of sugar and salts) and chloroplasts (contain chlorophyll used for photosynthesis).

Plants

- Plants make their own food through photosynthesis. Photosynthesis is a chemical reaction which happens in the green parts of plants, mainly the leaves, which contain chlorophyl. Photosynthesis can be represented by the following equation:

$$\text{Carbon dioxide} + \text{Water} \xrightarrow[\text{CHLOROPHYLL}]{\text{SUNLIGHT}} \text{Glucose} + \text{Oxygen}$$

- Flowers contain the plant's reproductive organs. The male part is the stamen which consists of the anther (with pollen) and the filament. The female part is the carpel consisting of the stigma, style and ovary. (Note: See Copy Master 2 for a diagram of a flowering plant.)
- To produce seeds pollen must be transferred from a stamen to a stigma. This can occur through self pollination, within the same plant or cross-pollination where the pollen from the stamen of one plant is transferred to the stigma of a different plant.
- Fertilisation occurs between a nucleus from pollen and the nucleus from an ovum. The ovary then develops into a fruit.
- Seeds can be dispersed by the wind, by animals and by explosions.

Atoms

- There are about 100 different sorts of atoms. Substances that contain only one sort of atom are 'elements'. Examples of elements are hydrogen, carbon and copper.
- Atoms can join together in a number of different ways to form different substances that have a variety of different properties.
- The size of particles and the forces of attraction between them determine whether the substance is a solid, liquid or gas at a particular temperature, and the temperature at which a substance melts or boils.

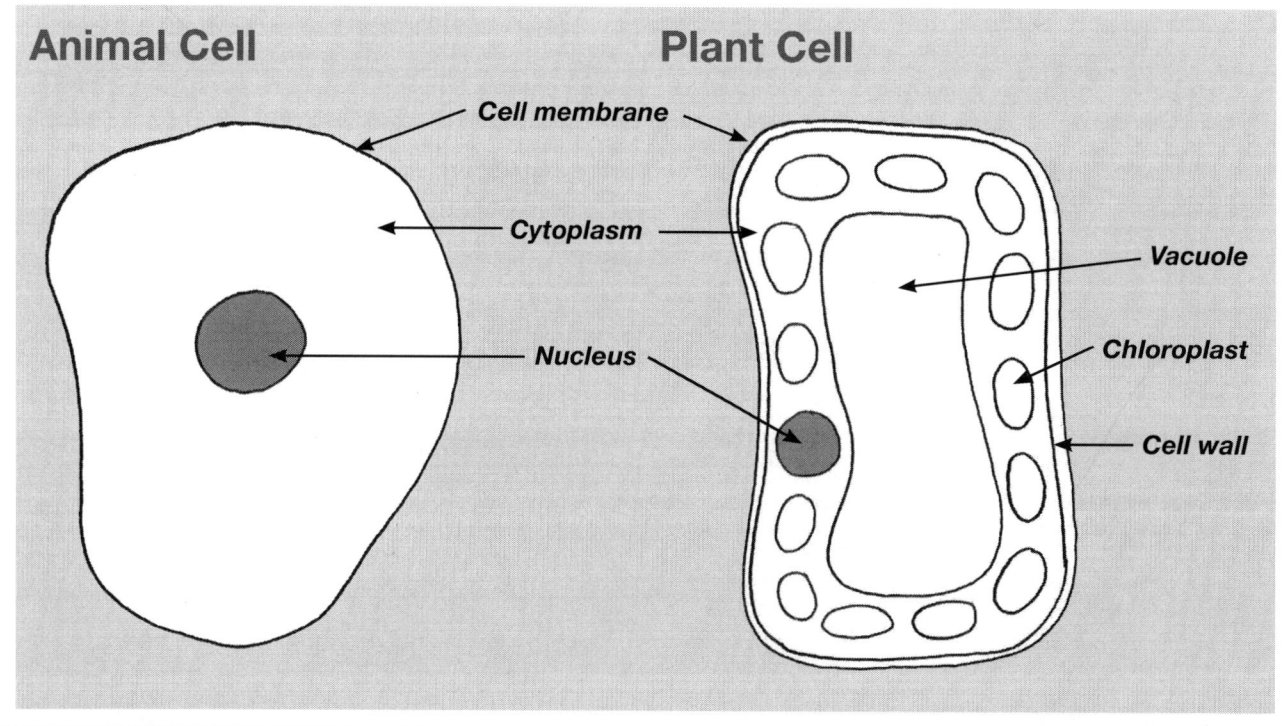

Solids, liquids and gases
- Solids maintain their own fixed shape and volume.
- Liquids have their own volume but take on the shape of their container. They retain a level surface. Finely powdered solids, like icing sugar and sand, may seem to behave like liquids when they are poured and take on the container's shape. The surface however will not remain horizontal if the container is tipped. This is different from a liquid's behaviour.
- Gases take on the shape and volume of their container.

Forces
- A force is a push or a pull. A twist is a combination of a push and pull.
- A body at rest remains at rest, and a body in motion continues in motion travelling in a straight line, unless acted on by a resultant force. (Newton's First Law').
- If a force acts on a body, an equal and opposite force acts on another body.
- Forces can make objects do five things: speed up; slow down; change direction; change shape; turn.
- Balanced forces produce no change in movement. E.g. An object floats when the downward force due to gravity is balanced by the upthrust resulting from the weight of water displaced.

Magnets
- Magnets attract iron, steel, nickel and cobalt.
- Each magnet has a North and a South pole.
- Magnets are strongest at the poles.
- Like poles repel.
- Unlike poles attract.
- If a magnet breaks, each piece becomes a magnet with a North and a South pole.

Energy
- There are eight main types of energy, namely: electrical, light, sound, kinetic/movement, thermal/heat; gravitational potential; chemical and elastic.
- The principle of 'Conservation of Energy' states that energy can never be created or destroyed. Instead energy is converted from one form to another.

Electricity
- Metals are conductors of electricity.
- Insulators do not conduct electricity. Examples include wood, plastic and rubber.
- Electricity will only flow if there is a complete circuit.
- In a circuit the cell, or battery (two or more cells), provides the force to push the electric charge around the circuit.
- For practical work, if a circuit appears not to work check:
  No loose or broken wires
  Bulbs are screwed in correctly and not blown
  No short circuits
  Cells are not 'dead'
  Cells provide the correct voltage for the components
- If doing an experiment to compare the 'brightness' of bulbs, ensure they are from the same manufacturer and the same type.

Light
- Light travels faster than sound.
- Light travels in straight lines.
- Light is produced by luminous objects. It reflects off non-luminous objects.
- We see when the light reflected from objects enters our eyes.
- When light travels from one transparent medium to another (e.g. light enters a block of glass) it bends or refracts.
- Light can travel through a vacuum.

Sound
- Sound is caused by something vibrating.
- Sound requires a medium to travel.
- Sound travels faster in solids than liquids, and faster in liquids than gases.
- The pitch of a sound depends on the frequency of vibration. Low-pitched notes are caused when something vibrates slowly. High-pitched notes are caused by something vibrating at a high speed.
- Sound waves travel more slowly than light waves. Thus we see lightning before thunder is heard.
- Humans can hear sounds in the range 20 vibrations/second to 1500 vibrations/second. Dogs and bats can hear sounds above 1500 vibrations/second.
- Loudness is determined by pressure on the ear. The closer we stand to a sound source the louder it will seem to be.
- Sound intensity is measured in decibels. One decibel is the smallest change in sound level that a human can detect.

Glossary for Life and Living Things

carnivore	Animals, and occasionally plants, that gain nutrients through consuming other animals.
chlorophyll	Green substance in plants that can absorb energy from sunlight and make it available for photosynthesis to take place.
digestion	The chemical and physical breaking down of food.
ecosystem	A community of living things and their habitat.

excrete	The way animals and plants get rid of waste, gas and water.
food chain	A diagram to show the feeding relationships within an ecosystem. The arrow represents the flow of energy.
food web	A diagram to show the inter-relationship of two or more food chains within an ecosystem.
fruit	Fleshy part surrounding the seed e.g. apple, tomato.
habitat	The environment for a group of animals and plants that provides all, or the majority, of needs for the inhabitants. These include the temperature, moisture, food, shelter and conditions to breed.
herbivore	An animal that consumes and gains nutrients from plants.
omnivore	An animal that consumes gains nutrients from plants and animals.
photosynthesis	The process by which plants make their own food.
pollination	The transfer of pollen from the anther to the stigma of a plant.
predator	An animal that gets its nutrients from consuming other animals.
prey	The food source (animal) for a predator.

Glossary for Materials

atom	Smallest particle that has the properties of the element from which it comes.
cluster	A small group of atoms/molecules.
condense	Change in phase from gas to liquid.
dissolve	Process of making a solution in which at least one of the chemicals is in a liquid state.
element	Material containing only one type of atom.
evaporate	Change in phase from liquid to gas.
freeze	Change in phase from liquid to solid.
gas	A state of matter that completely fills its container and can be compressed. In an ideal gas there are no interactions between neighbouring atoms/molecules.
insoluble	When particles cannot dissolve.
liquid	A state of matter that takes up the shape of its container and can be compressed a little. There are interactions between neighbouring atoms/molecules but no regular, long range, ordering of the particles.
mass	The amount of 'stuff'/substance measured in grams/kilograms.
material	Anything that has mass.
melt	Change in phase from solid to liquid.
metal	An element that is a good conductor of electricity.
mixture	Different elements/compounds mixed together with no chemical reaction between them.
molecule	Two or more atoms bonded together.
solid	A state of matter that holds its own shape. There are interactions between neighbouring atoms/molecules and regular ordering of the particles.
solidify	Change in phase from liquid to solid.
soluble	A solid is said to be soluble when it can dissolve.
solution	A mixture of chemicals, of which one at least is in a liquid state.
sublimation	Change in state from a solid to a gas without going through the liquid state.
suspension	When small particles of solid do not dissolve in a liquid but are distributed through the liquid.
vapour	An intermediate state between gas and liquid in which there are weak interactions between neighbouring atoms/molecules.

Glossary for Energy, Movement and Forces

air resistance	A type of friction (see friction).
amp	The unit of electric current.
battery	A group of cells.
cell	A container that has chemicals which react together to cause a flow of electrons from one terminal to another. (Note: A 'cell' is often called a 'battery' in everyday life. Within science, however, a battery is two or more cells.)
conductor	An electrical conductor is a material which allows electricity to flow through it. A thermal conductor is one which conducts heat.
force	A push or a pull. A twist is a combination of a push and a pull.
friction	A force that opposes motion between two surfaces. Friction includes air and water resistance.
insulator	An electrical insulator is a material that does not allow electricity to flow through it. Thermal insulation decreases the flow of heat. Sound insulation inhibits the transfer of sound. secondary light source A secondary light source is one that scatters or reflects lights from a primary source. e.g. the Moon which reflects light from the Sun.
SI units	An internationally agreed system for measurements commonly used within science where metre (m), kilogram (kg) and second (s) are the basic units. Agreed conventions for writing the symbols include: capitals are only used where the unit is named for someone (e.g. N for newton named after Isaac Newton); the letter 's' is never used for plurals (e.g. 'Ten metres' is written as '10m').
velocity	The speed of something in a given direction.
vibration	Regular movement backwards and forwards. Sound is the transfer of energy through vibrations of a medium.
volt	The unit of potential, which reflects the ability of a cell to do work.
weight	The force due to the pull of gravity, measured in newtons. On the Earth, 1 kilogram weighs approximately 10 newtons. On the Moon where the pull due to gravity is less, the weight would be smaller. (Note: In everyday life people often use the word 'weight' when describing how heavy an object is in kilograms. Scientifically, however, mass is measured in kilograms and weight is the force in newtons.)

Electrical Component	Symbol	Electrical Component	Symbol
bulb	—⊗—	buzzer	⌒
cell	—|⊢—	connector	———
motor	—(M)—	switch open switch closed	⁄ —

Planning to teach Science in the Primary Classroom

Copy Master 1

PHOTOCOPIABLE

Name: _____

Planning my investigation

These are the things that I can change or vary.

Deciding what to do

- *I will change*

- *I will observe/measure*

These are the things that I will keep the same

PHOTOCOPIABLE

Plant parts

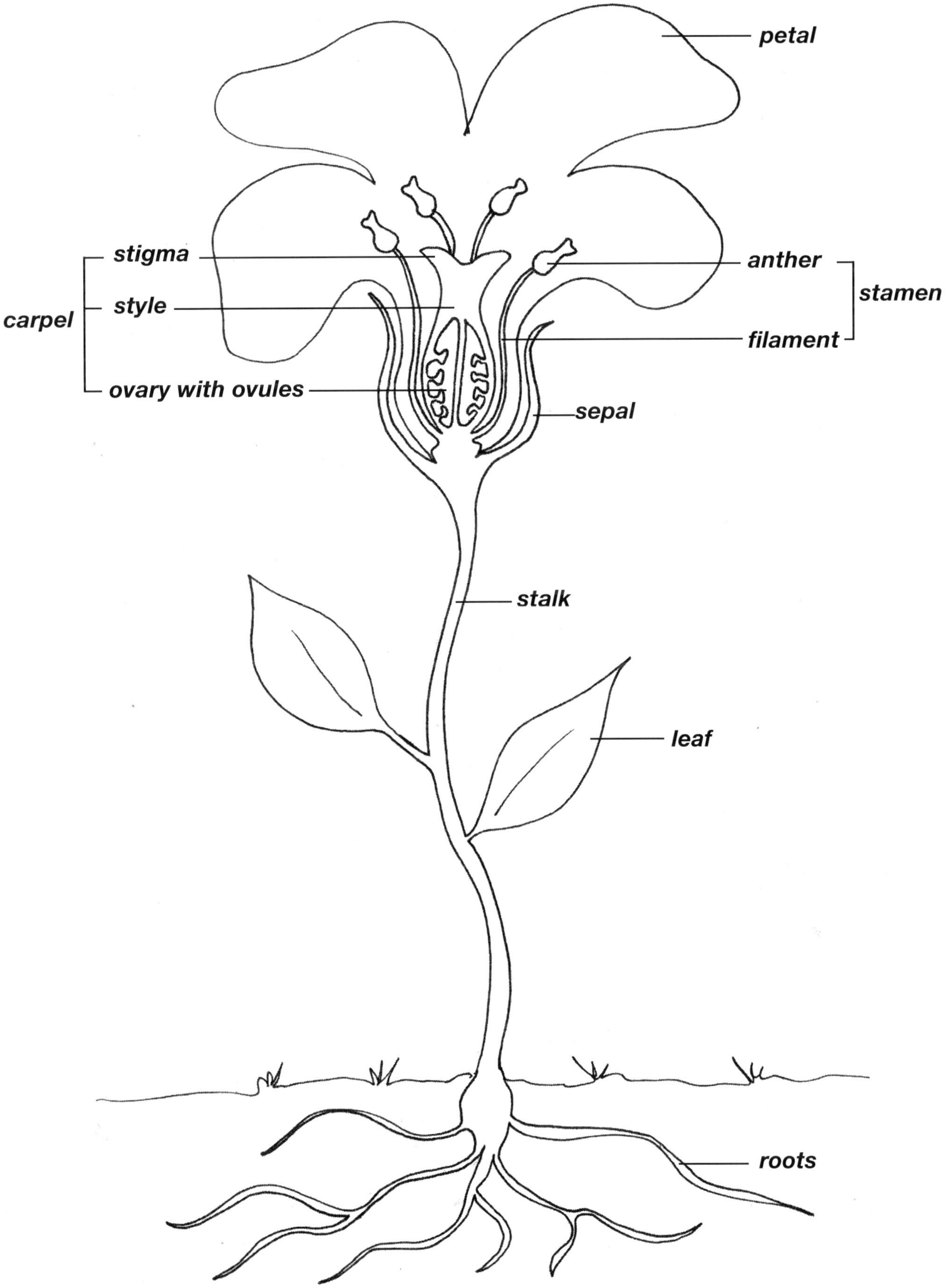

- petal
- stigma
- style
- ovary with ovules
- carpel
- anther
- filament
- stamen
- sepal
- stalk
- leaf
- roots

Copy Master 3

PHOTOCOPIABLE

Human digestive system

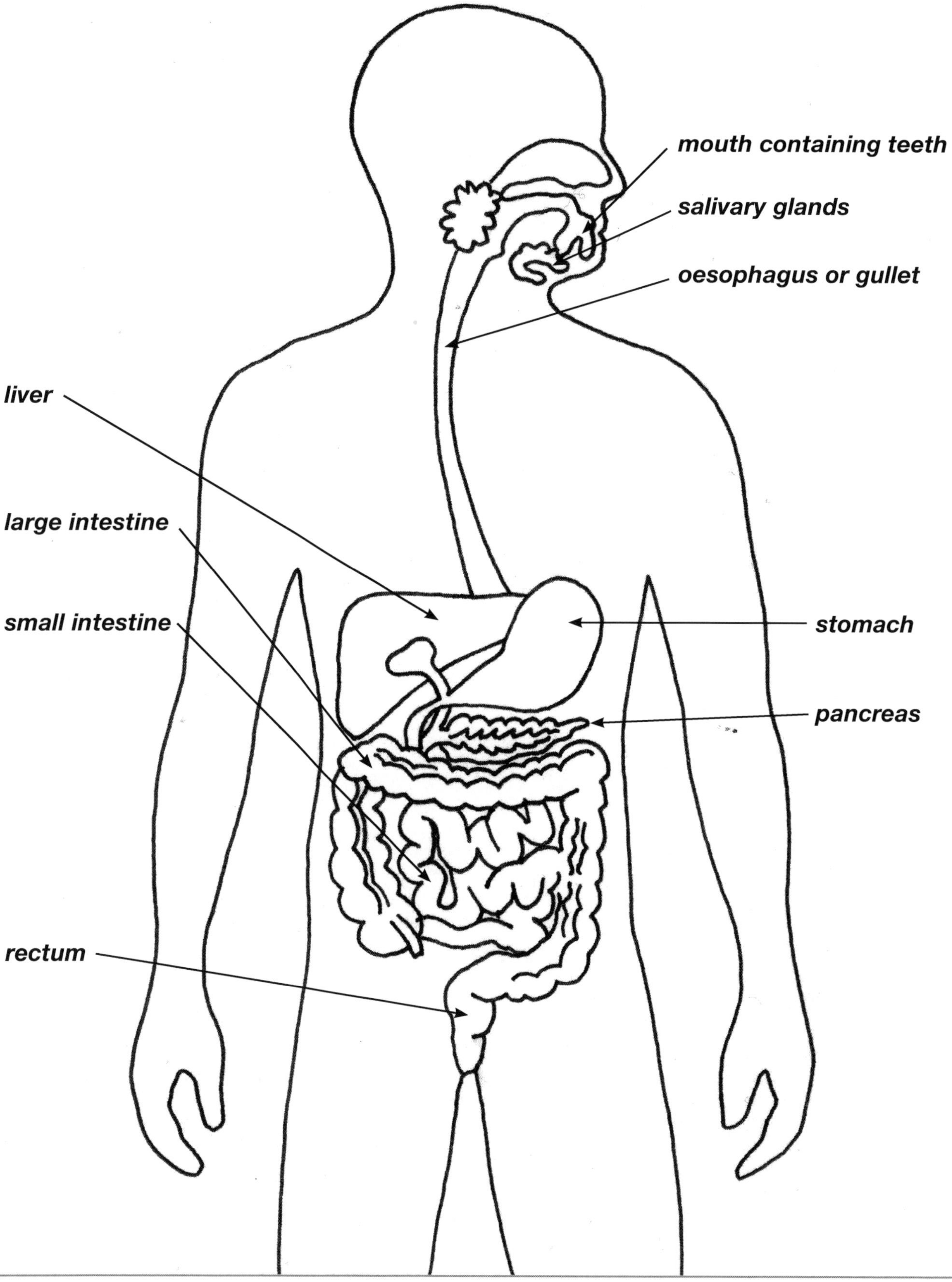

- mouth containing teeth
- salivary glands
- oesophagus or gullet
- liver
- large intestine
- small intestine
- stomach
- pancreas
- rectum

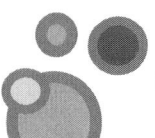

PHOTOCOPIABLE

Copy Master 4

Human body skeleton

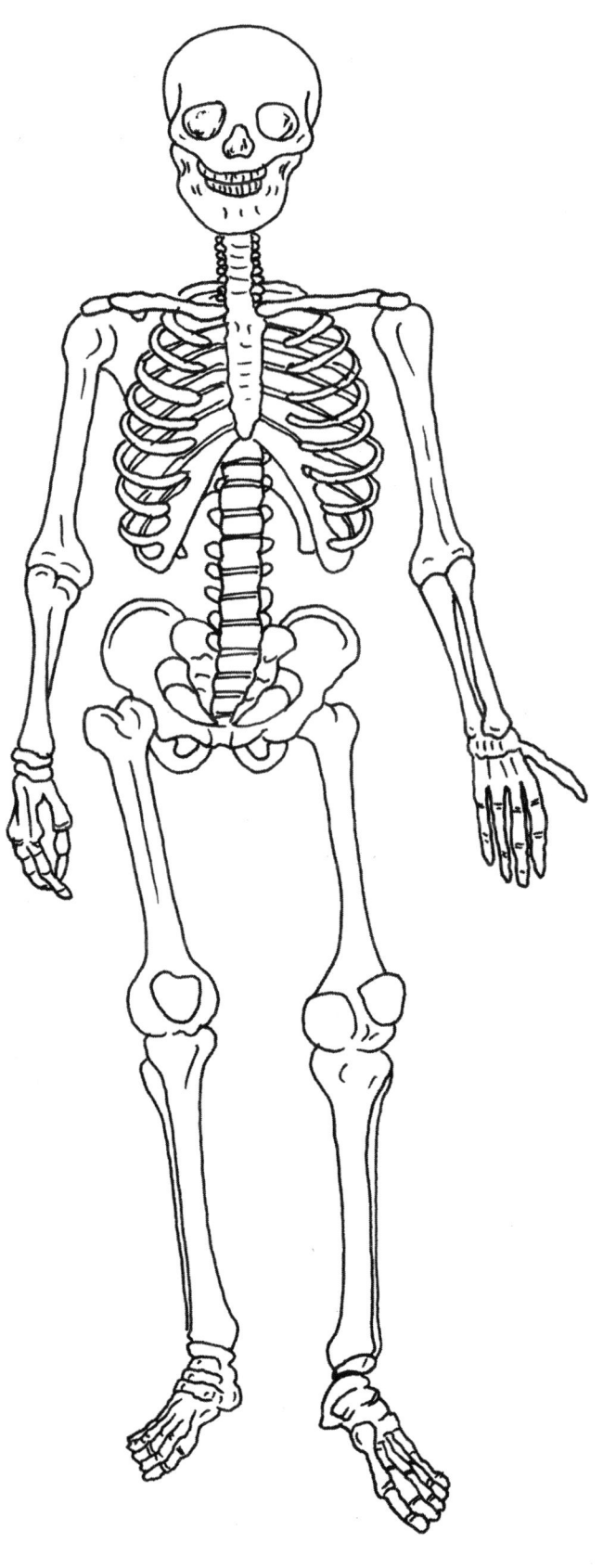

Copy Master 5

PHOTOCOPIABLE

Inside the human eye and ear

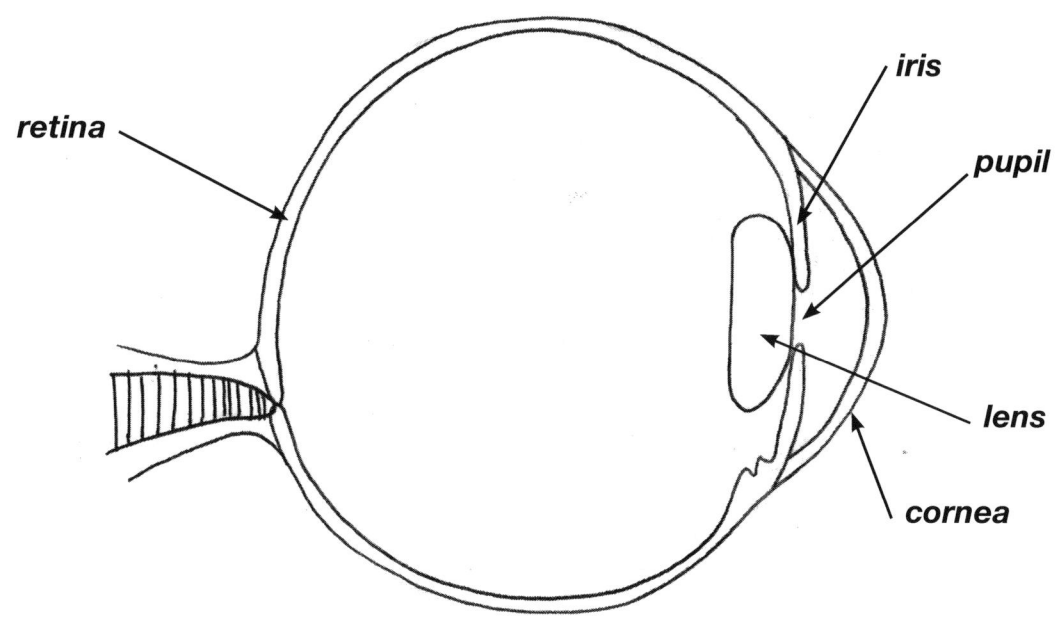

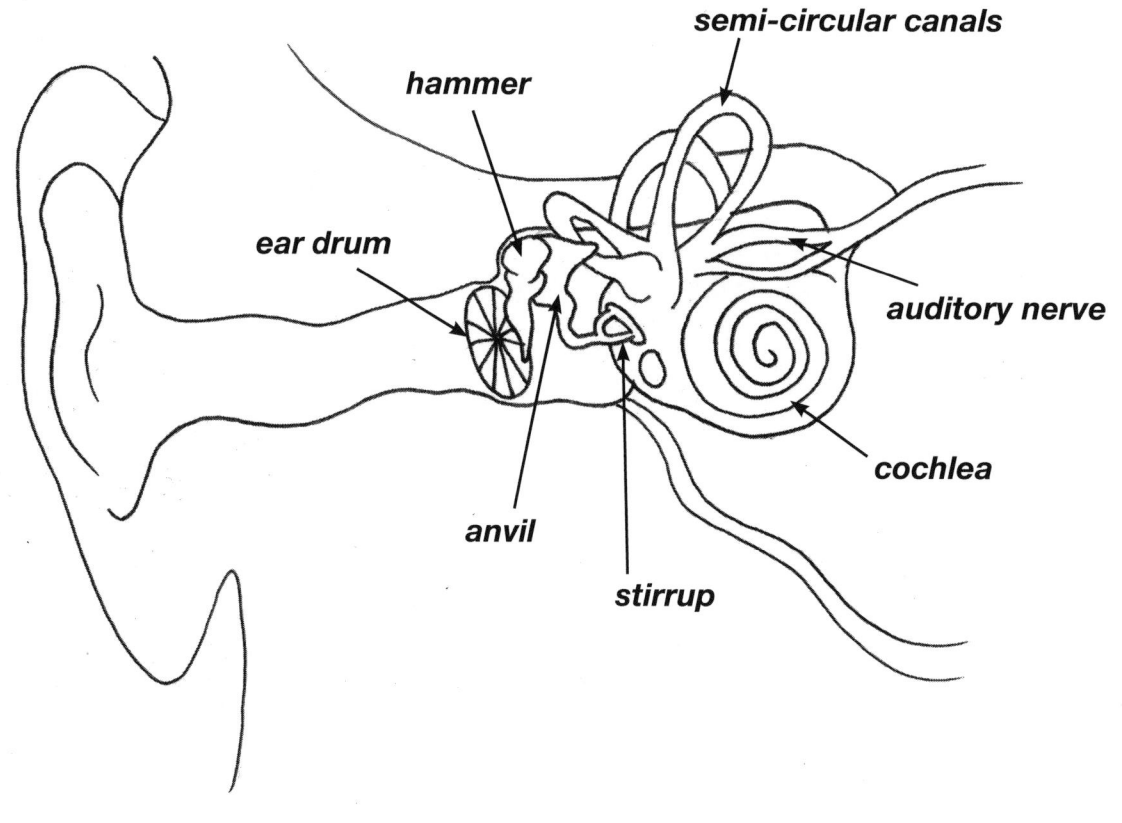

Copy Master 6

PHOTOCOPIABLE

Human teeth

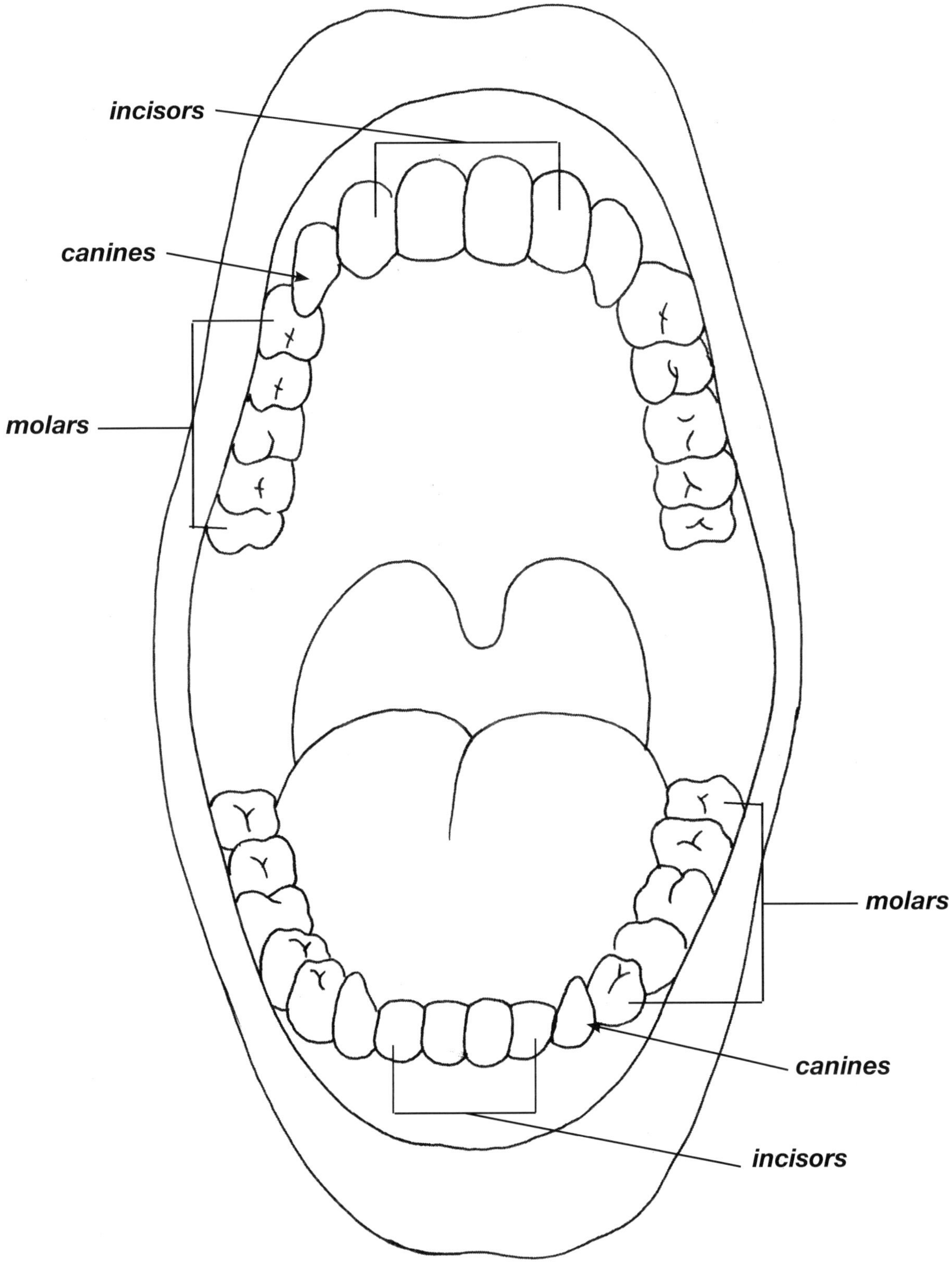

- incisors
- canines
- molars
- molars
- canines
- incisors

Planning to teach Science in the Primary Classroom

Section Four 37

Copy Master 7

PHOTOCOPIABLE

Living or never been alive?

PHOTOCOPIABLE

Name:

Where do minibeasts live?

Place a tick in the table to show where the minibeasts were found.

Minibeast	On a plant	Under a stone	Under a log	In the air	On a path	Other

Copy Master 9

PHOTOCOPIABLE

Name:

Balanced Eating

- Fruit and vegetables
- Bread, rice, potatoes, pasta
- Milk and dairy foods
- Foods and drinks high in fat and/or sugar.
- Meat, fish, eggs, beans and other non-dairy sources of protein

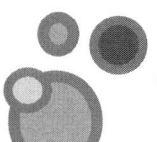

Copy Master 10

PHOTOCOPIABLE

Identifying leaves

 ash	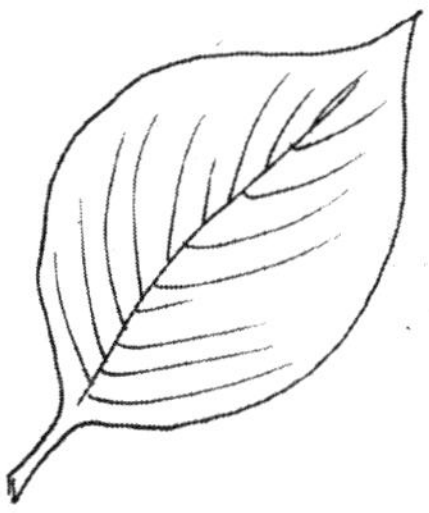 beech	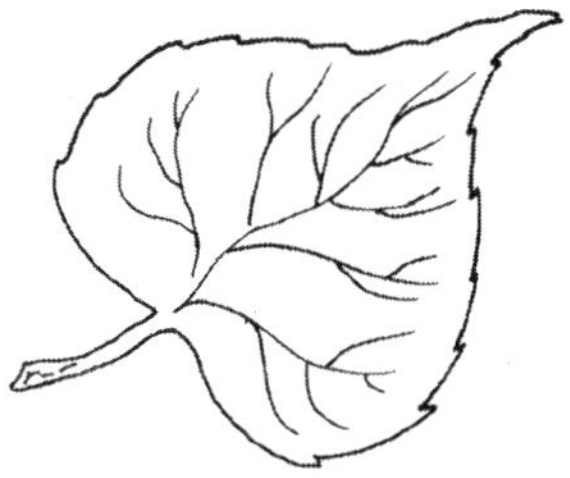 common lime
 fir	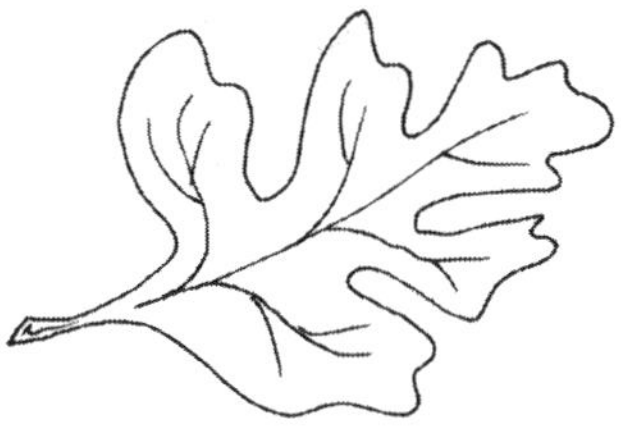 hawthorn	 holly
 horse chestnut	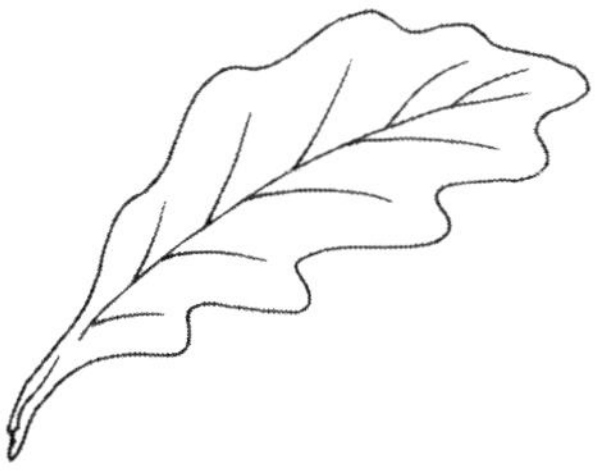 oak	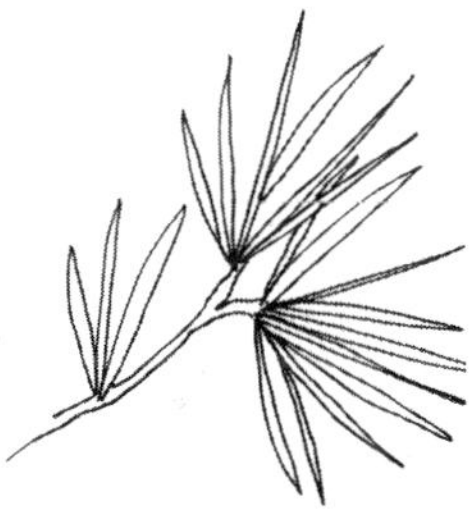 pine
 plane	 silver birch	 sweet chestnut
 sycamore	 wild cherry	 yew

Planning to teach Science in the Primary Classroom

Section Four 41

Copy Master 11

PHOTOCOPIABLE

Identifying plants

 campion (red/white)	 chickweed	 common St John's wort
 creeping buttercup	 dead nettle	 dog violet
 forget-me-not	 golden rod	 greater bindweed
 heather	 hedge parsley	 lesser celandine
 poppy	 primrose	 wood sorrel

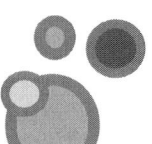

Copy Master 12

PHOTOCOPIABLE

Identifying minibeasts

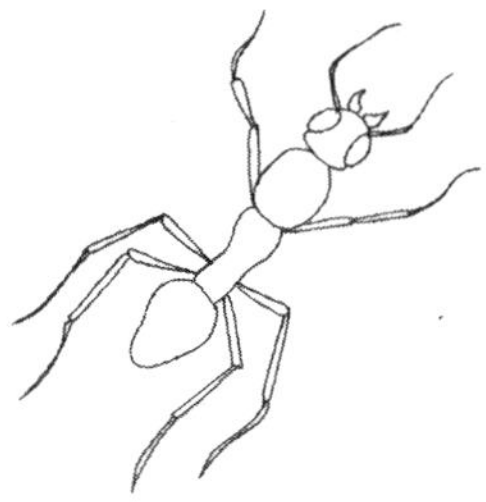 ant	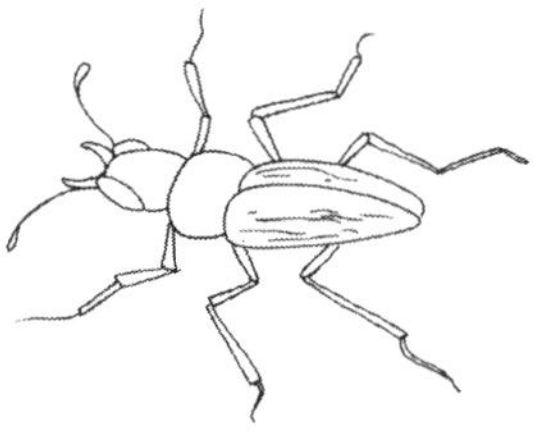 beetle	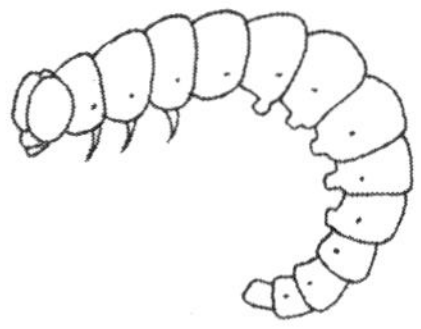 caterpillar
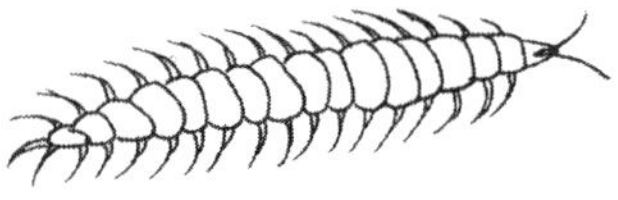 centipede	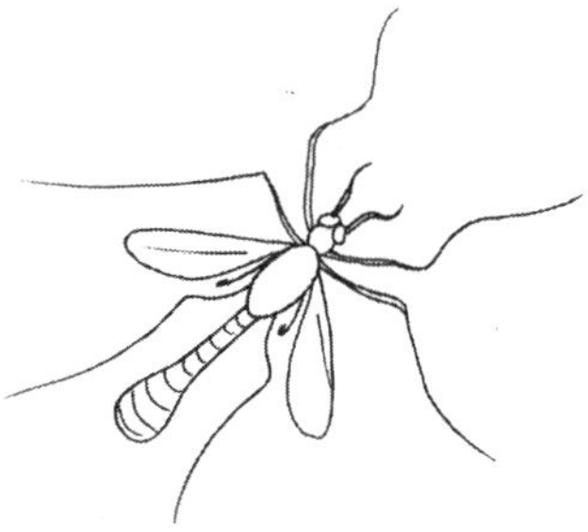 crane-fly	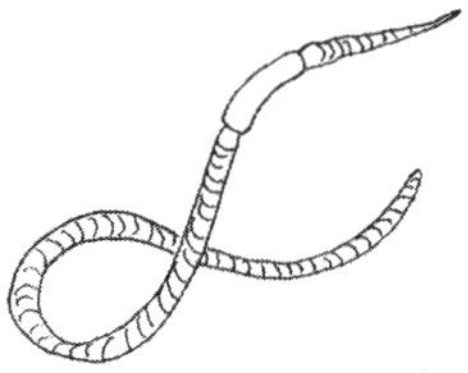 earthworm
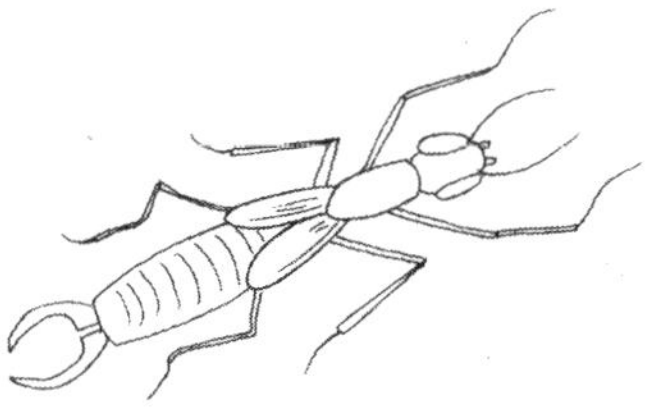 earwig	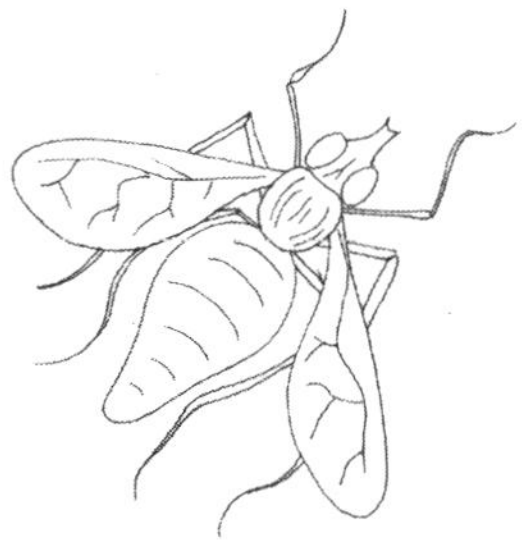 fly	 ladybird
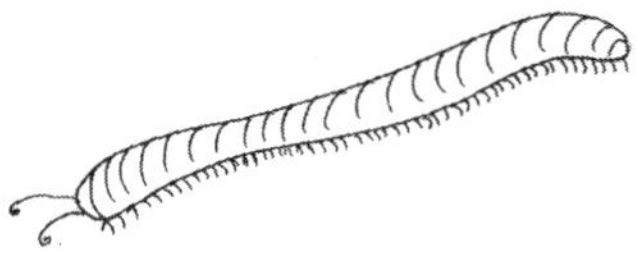 millipede	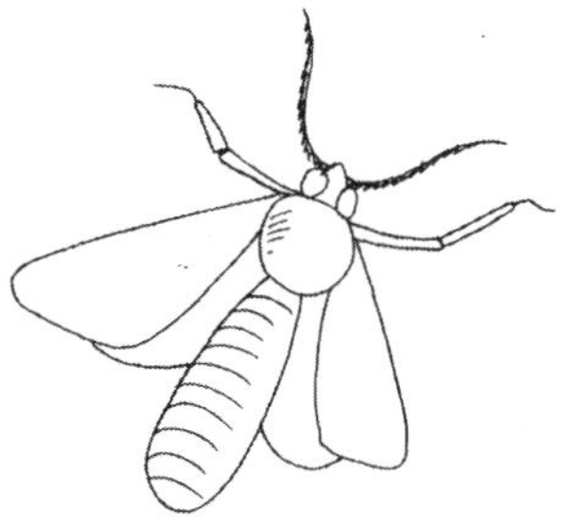 moth	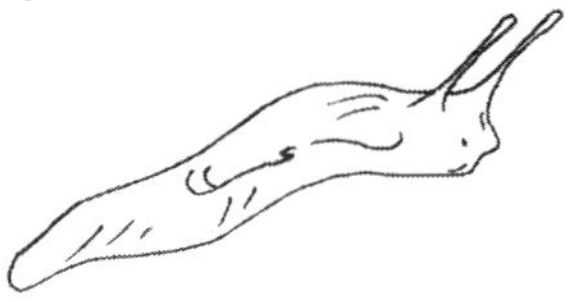 slug
 snail	 spider	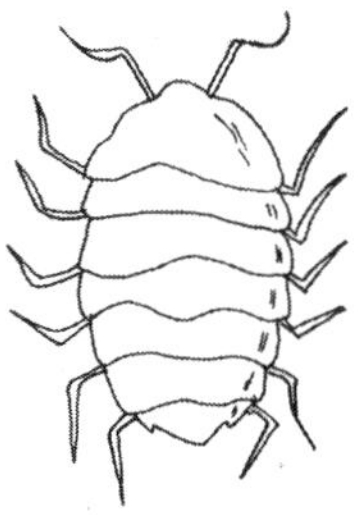 woodlouse

Planning to teach Science in the Primary Classroom

Copy Master 13

PHOTOCOPIABLE

Identifying pond creatures

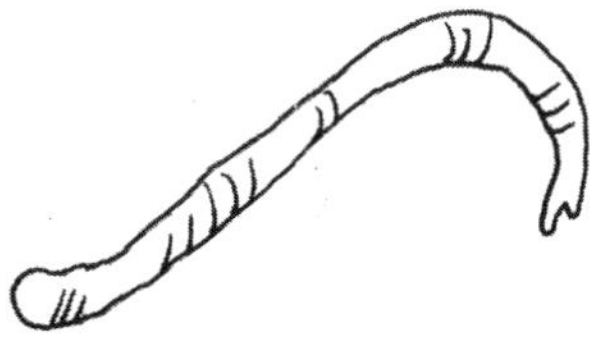 **bloodworm**	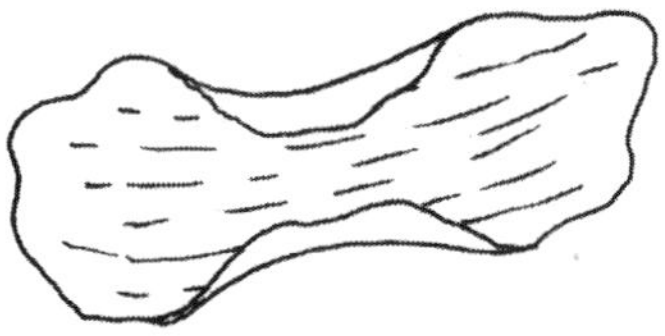 **flatworm**	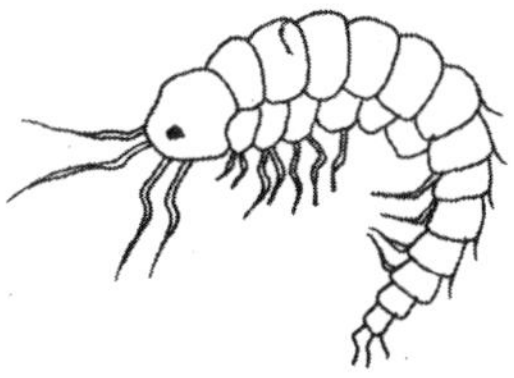 **freshwater shrimp**
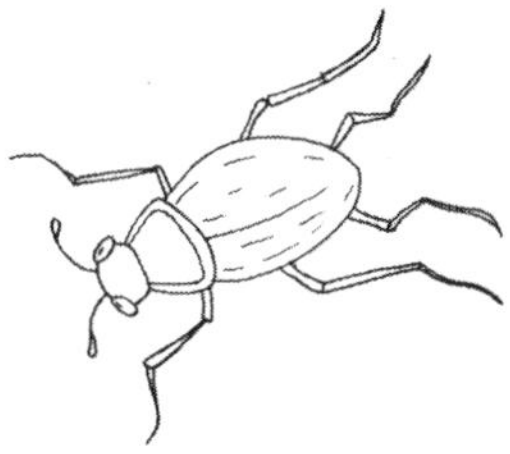 **great diving beetle**	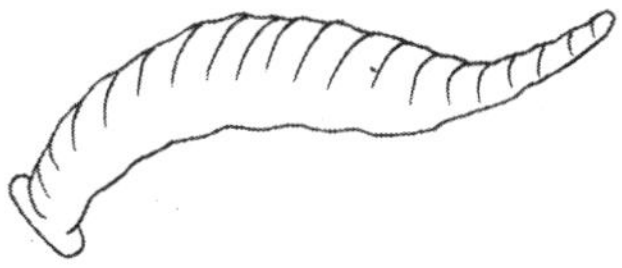 **leech**	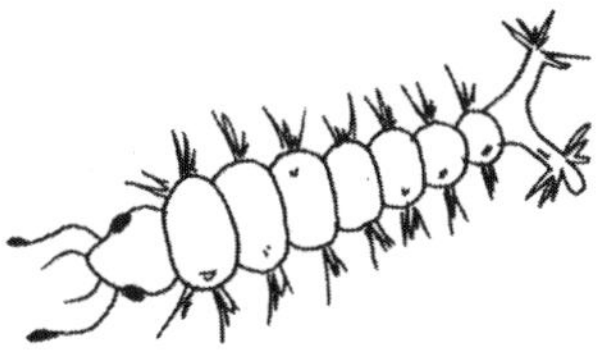 **mosquito larva**
 **mosquito pupa**	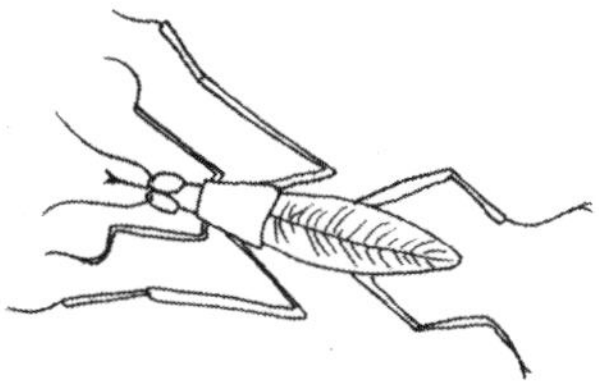 **pond skater**	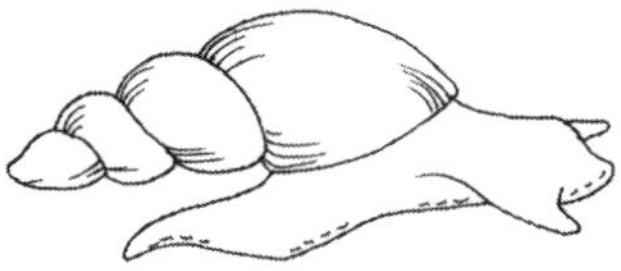 **pond snail**
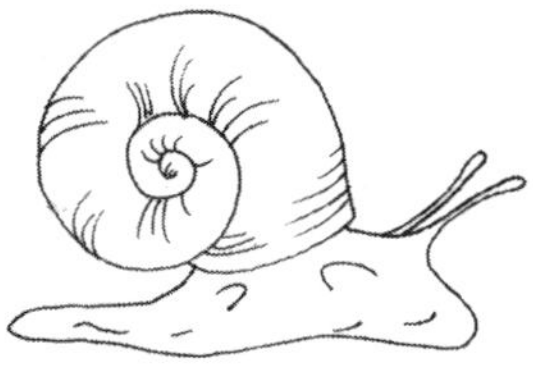 **ram's-horn snail**	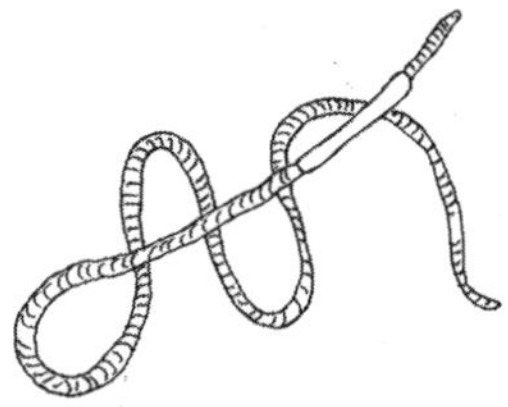 **sludgeworm**	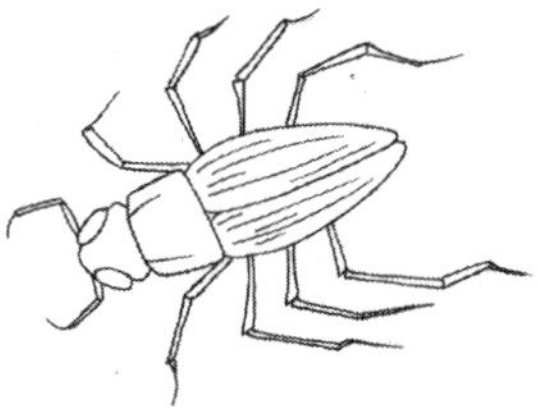 **water beetle**
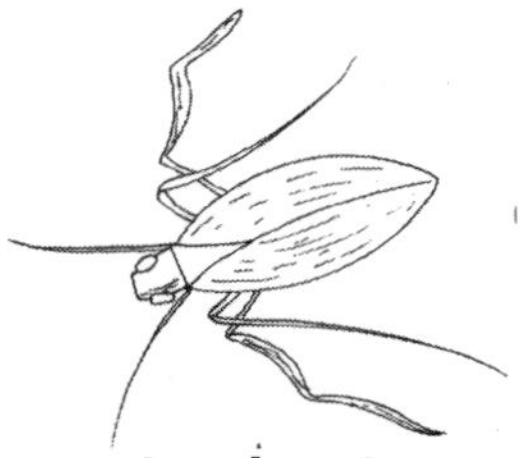 **water-boatman**	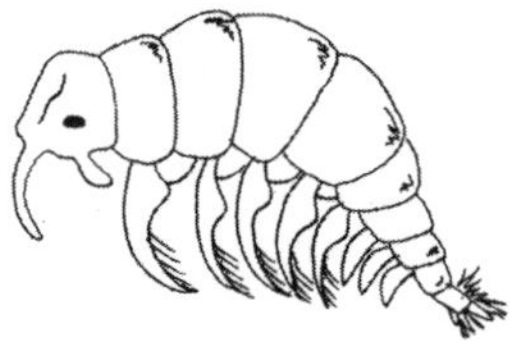 **water flea**	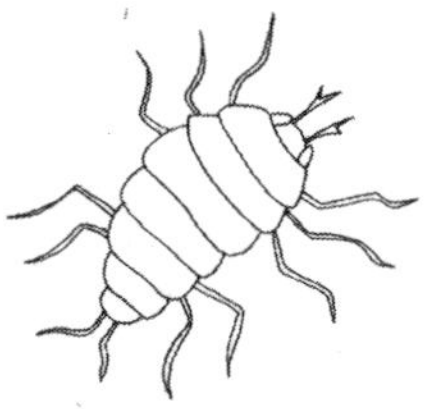 **water louse**
 **water mite**	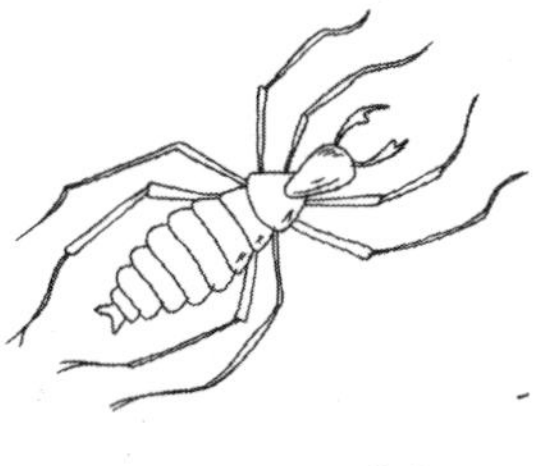 **water spider**	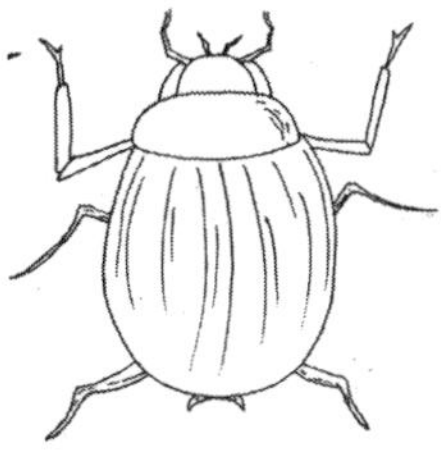 **whirligig beetle**

44 Section Four

Planning to teach Science in the Primary Classroom

Making paper 'seeds'

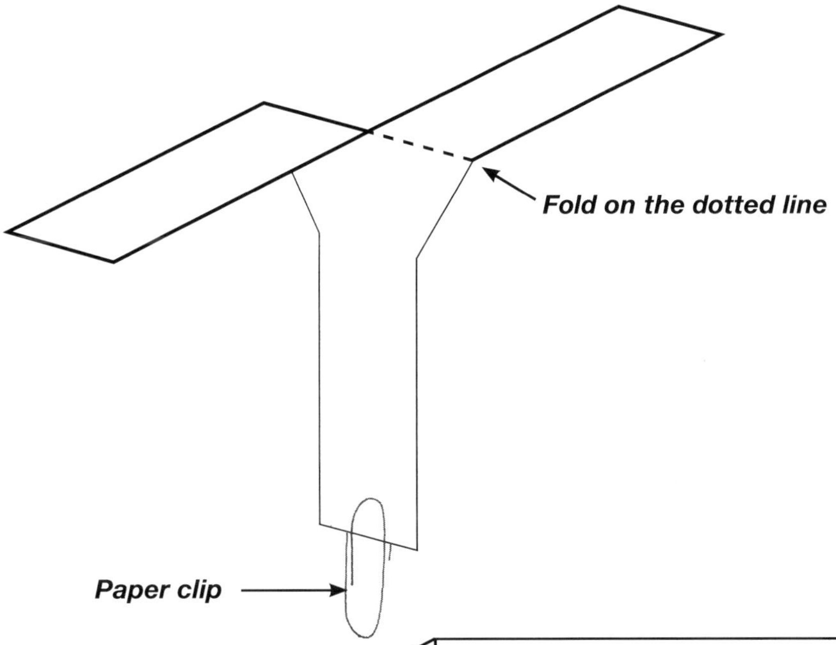

Fold on the dotted line

Paper clip

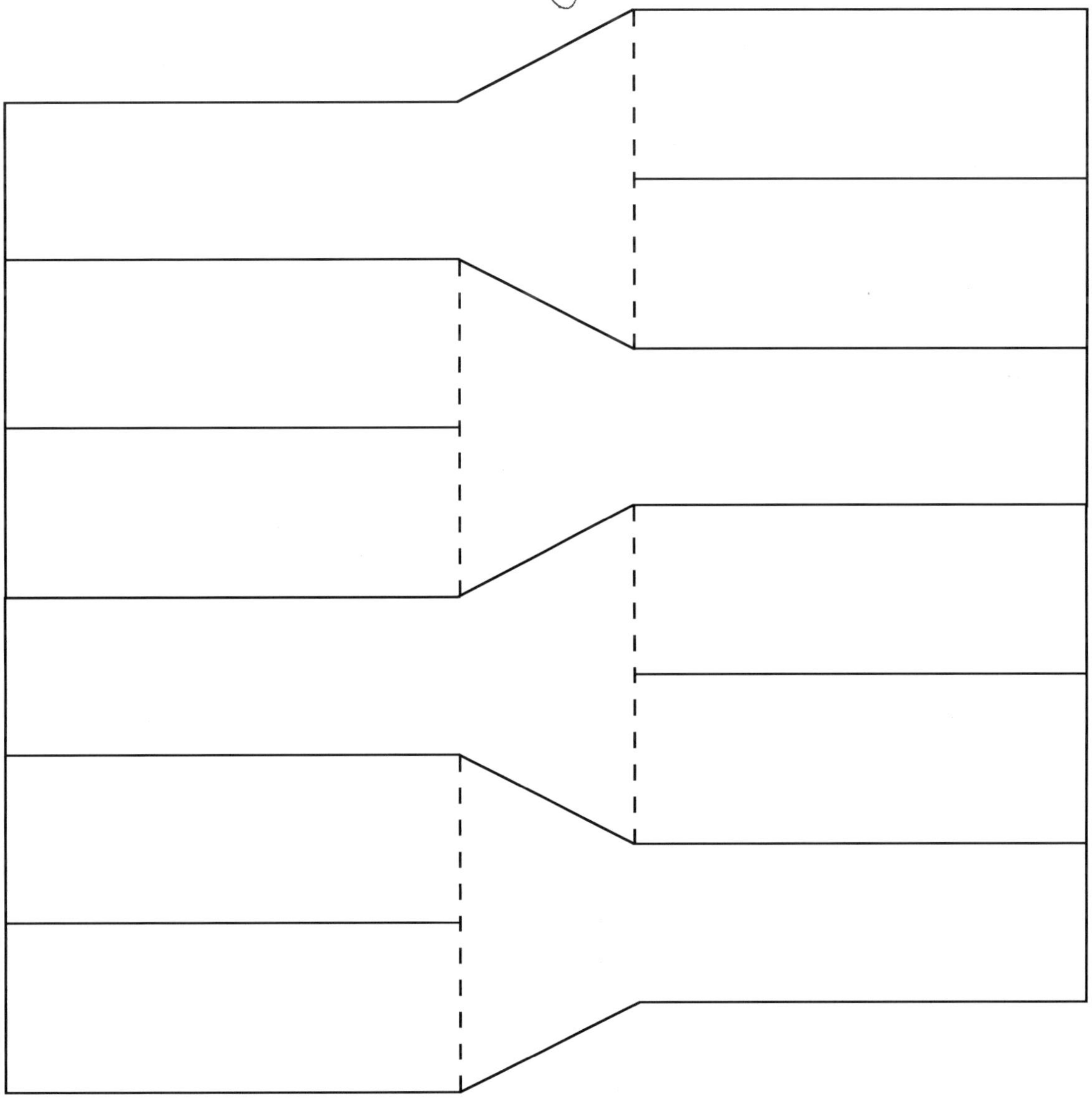

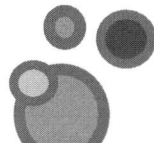

Copy Master 15

PHOTOCOPIABLE

Germinating seed flick book

The germination of a seed

by _____

Name:_____

Gas, Liquid or Solid?

Think about each of the materials in the table. Tick whether you think it is a gas, a liquid or a solid at room temperature. Be prepared to give reasons for your answer!

Material	Gas	Liquid	Solid
Chocolate			
Golden Syrup			
Sand			
Hair mousse			
Paint			
Water			
Toothpaste			
Spray polish			
Flour			
Hot chocolate			
Helium in a balloon			
Milk			
Jelly			
Ice cream			
Paper			
Wood			
Honey			
Bubbles in a fizzy drink			
Glass			

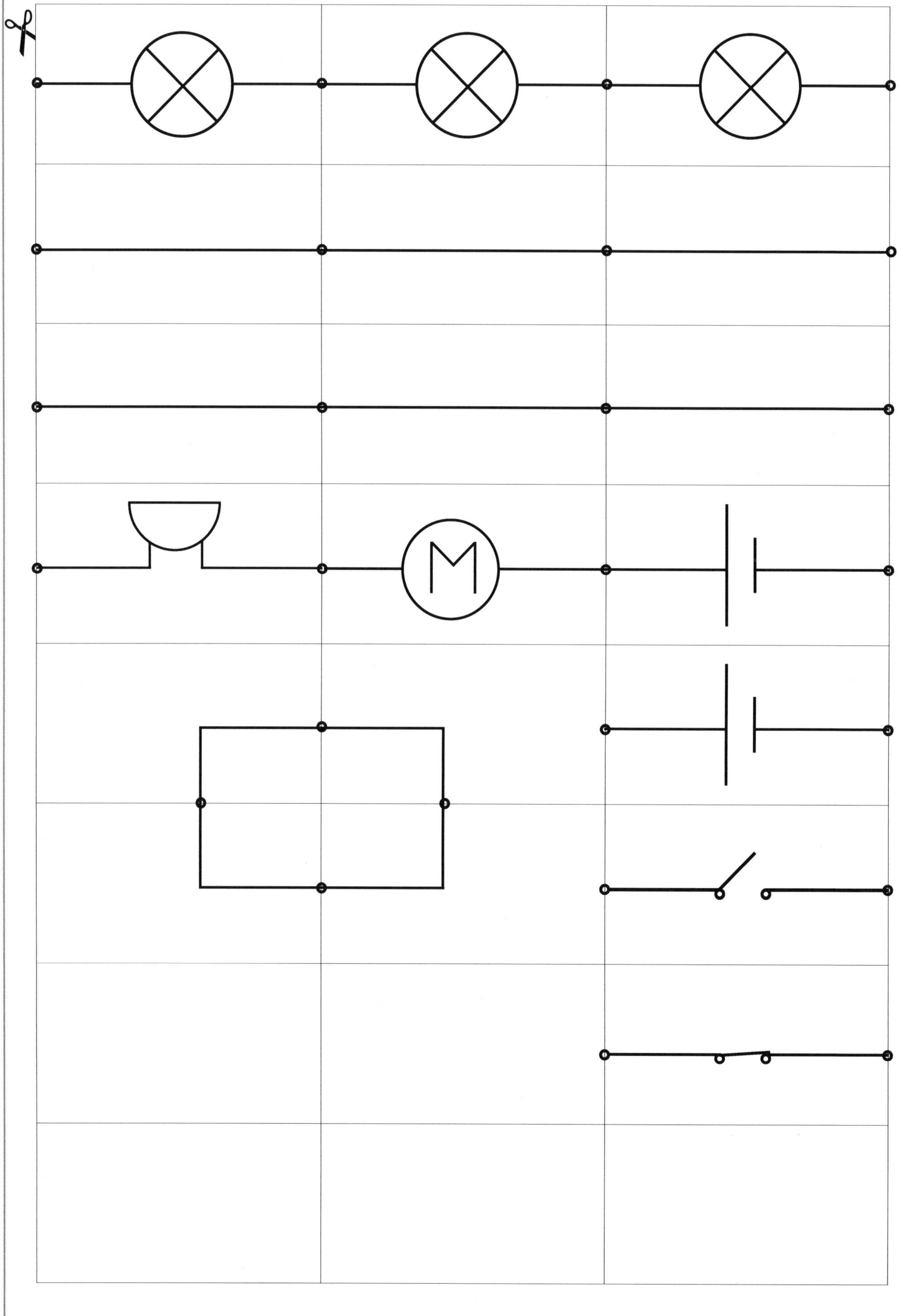

Copy Master 18

PHOTOCOPIABLE

Musical Instruments

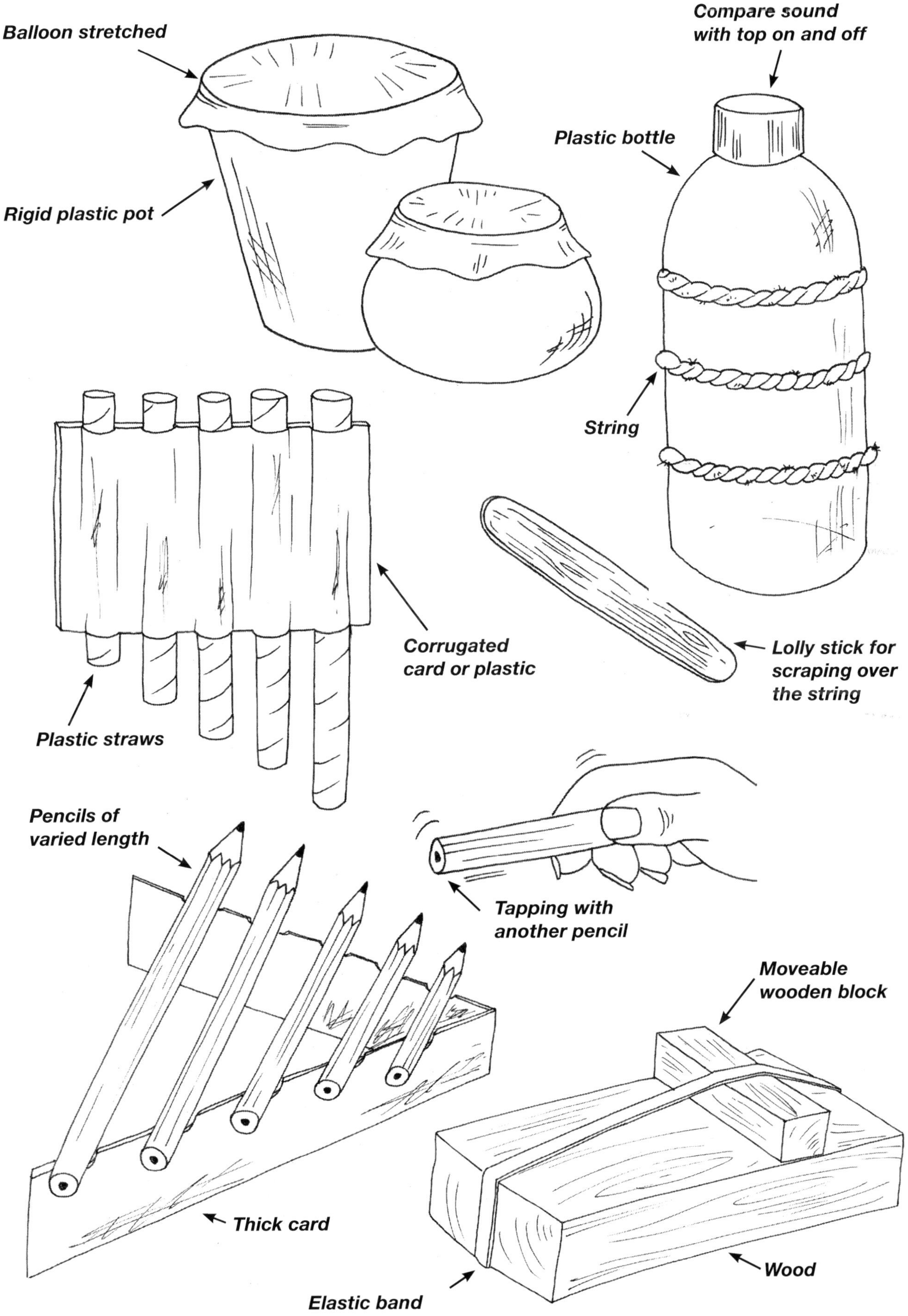

- Balloon stretched
- Rigid plastic pot
- Compare sound with top on and off
- Plastic bottle
- String
- Corrugated card or plastic
- Plastic straws
- Lolly stick for scraping over the string
- Pencils of varied length
- Tapping with another pencil
- Moveable wooden block
- Thick card
- Elastic band
- Wood

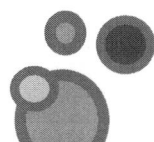

Copy Master 19

PHOTOCOPIABLE

_____'s glossary on_____

Word	Definition

Did you know?

Human body facts

- There are more than 50,000,000,000,000 cells in a human body and 100,000 of them can fit on the head of a pin.
- Your heart beats about 100,000 times a day.
- Sneezes leave our mouths at a speed of about 160 kilometres per hour.
- It is impossible to sneeze with your eyes open.

Animal facts

- A flea can jump 130 times higher than its own height. This is the same as a person of height 154 centimetres being able to jump 200 metres in the air!

- A cricket's ears can be found on the front legs just below the knees.

- Bats cannot walk because their leg muscles are very thin.

Plant facts

- A sunflower contains about 1000 seeds.

- Each floret in a dandelion head becomes a seed if it is pollinated. A dandelion plant can make up to 500 seeds.

Space facts

- If we travelled at the speed of light we could go: 8 times round the world in a second; to the Moon and back in 3 seconds; to Jupiter in three hours.

Sound facts

- Humans can hear sounds in the range 20 vibrations/second to 1500 vibrations/second.

- Dogs and bats can hear sounds above 1500 vibrations/second.

- 80 decibels is the level of sound intensity at which hearing protection must be worn in a work place. (A fridge would register about 40dB whilst an emergency vehicle siren might be about 120dB. 0dB is the threshold for hearing.)

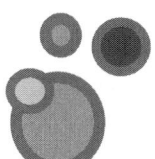

Table to show how the activities relate to the QCA Units of Work for Science

PHOTOCOPIABLE

Activity Area	QCA Unit Links
Life processes	Unit 1B: Growing plants Unit 2B: Plants and animals in the local environment Unit 3B: Helping plants grow well
Humans and other animals	Unit 1A: Ourselves
Senses	Unit 1F: Sound and hearing
Teeth	Unit 3A: Teeth and eating
Exercise and healthy diets	Unit 2A: Health and growth Unit 5A: Keeping healthy
Hearts	Unit 5A: Keeping healthy
Skeletons	Unit 4A: Moving and growing
Life cycles	Unit 5B: Life cycles
Drugs	Unit 5A: Keeping healthy
Green plants	Unit 1B: Growing plants Unit 3B: Helping plants grow well
Variation and classification	Unit 2C: Variation
Living things in their environment	Unit 2B: Plants and animals in the local environment
Feeding relationships	Unit 6A: Interdependence and adaptation
Micro-organisms	Unit 6B: Micro-organisms
Grouping and classifying materials	Unit 1C: Sorting and using materials Unit 2D: Grouping and changing materials Unit 3C: Characteristics of materials
Keeping warm	Unit 4C: Keeping warm
Rocks and soils	Unit 3D: Rocks and soils
Solids, liquids and gases	Unit 4D: Solids, liquids and how they can be separated
Changing materials	Unit 1C: Sorting and using materials Unit 2D: Grouping and changing materials Unit 3C: Characteristics of materials
Non-reversible changes	Unit 6D: Reversible and irreversible changes
Separating mixtures of materials	Unit 4D: Solids, liquids and how they can be separated
Electricity	Unit 2F: Using electricity Unit 4F: Circuits and conductors Unit 6G: Changing circuits
Forces and motion	Unit 1E: Pushes and pulls Unit 2E: Forces and movement
Magnets	Unit 3E: Magnets and springs
Friction	Unit 4E: Friction
Forces in action and measuring forces	Unit 6E: Forces in action
Light and dark	Unit 1D: Light and dark
Shadows	Unit 3F: Light and shadows
Reflecting light and seeing	Unit 6F: How we see things
Making and detecting sound	Unit 1F: Sound and hearing
Changing sounds and hearing	Unit 5F: Changing sounds
The Sun, Earth and Moon	Unit 5E: Earth, Sun and Moon
Periodic changes	Unit 5E: Earth, Sun and Moon

(Reference: http://www.standards.dfes.gov.uk/schemes2/science/)

Index

air resistance	25
anther	28, 33
assessment	10
atom	30
attract	24
auditory nerve	36
battery	31
bladder	34
bulb	23, 31
canine	37
carpel	28, 33
carnivore	29
cell	28, 31
chlorophyll	28, 29
classification	18, 20
cochlea	36
concept map	11
concepts	7
condense	30
conductor	23, 31
connector	31
controlling variables	8
cornea	36
cross-curricular links	12
dark	25
digestion	29
diets	16, 40
displays	12
drugs	17
ear drum	36
Earth	27
ecosystem	29
electricity	23, 31
element	30
energy	23, 29
evaporate	30
exercise	16
extension	13
fair test	8
food chain	19
food web	30
forces	23, 24, 29
freeze	30
friction	25
gas	30
glossary	10
habitat	19, 30
heart	17, 34
herbivore	30
ICT	12
incisor	37
individual needs	13
insoluble	30
insulator	20
investigation	7
iris (eye)	36
kidneys	34
large intestine	34
leaf	18, 33
lens	36
life cycles	17
life processes	15
light	25, 29
liquid	21, 29
liver	34
lungs	34
magnets	24, 29
mass	30
micro-organism	20
minibeast	18, 19, 39, 43
Moon	27
molar	37
motor	31
omnivore	30
ovary	33
ovule	33
petal	33
photosynthesis	30
planning	9
plants	17
plenary	9
pollination	30
ponds	15, 19
predator	30
prey	30
primary light source	25
pupil (eye)	36
QCA Scheme of Work	9, 52
recording	10
reflecting	26
rocks	21
root	33
safety	9, 14
scheme of work	9, 52
secondary light source	25
seeing	26
senses	16
separating	22
session plans	9
shadows	25
SI units	31
skeleton	17
skills	7
small intestine	34
soil	21
solid	21, 29
sound	26, 29, 49
space	27
stamen	33
stomach	34
style	33
Sun	27
teeth	16
variables	8
variation	18
vibration	26, 29, 31
weight	31

Planning to teach Science in the Primary Classroom